# getting culture

**the society pages**

*The Social Side of Politics*

*Crime and the Punished*

*Color Lines and Racial Angles*

*Owned*

the
society
pages

# getting culture

## douglas hartmann

UNIVERSITY OF MINNESOTA

## christopher uggen

UNIVERSITY OF MINNESOTA

w. w. norton & company

NEW YORK | LONDON

W. W. Norton & Company has been independent since its founding in 1923, when William Warder Norton and Mary D. Herter Norton first published lectures delivered at the People's Institute, the adult education division of New York City's Cooper Union. The firm soon expanded its program beyond the Institute, publishing books by celebrated academics from America and abroad. By mid-century, the two major pillars of Norton's publishing program—trade books and college texts—were firmly established. In the 1950s, the Norton family transferred control of the company to its employees, and today—with a staff of four hundred and a comparable number of trade, college, and professional titles published each year—W. W. Norton & Company stands as the largest and oldest publishing house owned wholly by its employees.

Book Design: Isaac Tobin
Composition: Westchester Book Composition
Manufacturing: Courier-Westford
Production Manager: Sean Mintus

ISBN: 978-0-393-92041-3

Library of Congress Cataloging-in-Publication Data

Hartmann, Douglas.
    Getting culture / Douglas Hartmann, University of Minnesota,
Christopher Uggen, University of Minnesota. — First Edition.
        pages cm. — (The society pages ; Volume 5)
    Includes bibliographical references and index.
    ISBN 978-0-393-92041-3 (pbk. : alk. paper)
    1. Culture.   I. Uggen, Christopher.   II. Title.
    HM621.H3735 2015
    306—dc23

                                             2015015328

W. W. Norton & Company, Inc., 500 Fifth Avenue, New York, NY 10110-0017
www.wwnorton.com
W. W. Norton & Company, Ltd., Castle House, 75/76 Wells Street, London
W1T3QT

# thesocietypages.org

# contents

**Series Preface**

    DOUGLAS HARTMANN AND CHRISTOPHER UGGEN   xi

**Introduction**

    DOUGLAS HARTMANN AND CHRISTOPHER UGGEN   xv

**Changing Lenses: Exploring Dora**

    DOUGLAS HARTMANN WITH WING YOUNG HUIE   xxv


## part 1   cultural sociology: how we think and what we do  1

### 1   Same Sex, Different Attitudes

KATHLEEN E. HULL   3

### 2   The Feel of Faith

DANIEL WINCHESTER   17

3    **Music and the Quest for a Tribe**
**with Jennifer C. Lena**
SARAH LAGESON   37

4    **All Together, Now: Producing Fashion**
**at the Global Level**
CLAUDIO E. BENZECRY   49

## part 2 sociological critiques of culture   73

5    **Troubling Bodies with Abigail Saguy, Natalie Boero,**
**and C. J. Pascoe**
KYLE GREEN   75

6    **The Homogenization of Asian Beauty**
C.N. LE   97

7    **Comic-Conned: Gender Norms in a Carnivalesque**
**Atmosphere**
NATALIE WILSON   113

8    **Burning Man with Katherine K. Chen, S. Megan**
**Heller, and Jon Stern**
MATT WRAY   129

# part 3 culture as ways of life: communities and lifestyles   153

9   **Together Alone with Eric Klinenberg**
ARTURO BAIOCCHI AND STEPHEN SUH   155

10  **Deep Play and Flying Rats with Colin Jerolmack**
KYLE GREEN   165

11  **Coded Chaos and Anonymous with Gabriella Coleman**
KYLE GREEN   181

12  **On Digital Austerity**
NATHAN JURGENSON   199

**Discussion Guide and Group Activities**   213
**About the Contributors**   219
**Index**   223

# series preface

**DOUGLAS HARTMANN AND CHRISTOPHER UGGEN**

It started with a conversation about record labels. Our favorite imprints are known for impeccable taste, creative design, and an eye for both quality and originality. Wouldn't it be cool if W. W. Norton & Company and TheSocietyPages.org joined forces to develop a book series with the same goals in mind? Namely, to consistently deliver the best work by the most original voices in the field.

The Society Pages (TSP) is a multidisciplinary online hub bringing fresh social scientific knowledge and insight to the broadest public audiences in the most open, accessible, and timely manner possible. The largest, most visible collection of sociological material on the web (currently drawing over 1 million readers per month), TSP is composed of a family of prolific blogs and bloggers, podcasts, interviews, exchanges, teaching content, reading recommendations, and original features like "There's Research on That!" (TROT), "Office Hours," "Citings & Sightings," and "The Reading List." The TSP book series, published in collaboration with W. W. Norton, assembles the best original content from the website in key thematic collections. With contributions from leading scholars and a provocative collection of discussion topics and group activities, this innovative series provides an accessible and affordable entry point for strong sociological perspectives on topics of immediate social import and public relevance.

The fifth volume in this series deals with culture, broadly and ecumenically defined. As in our previous volumes, the chapters are organized in three main sections; however, because definitions of culture vary almost as widely as the methods used to study culture, we tweaked the scheme just a bit. "Cultural Sociology" provides a sampling of the unique subjects, materials, and methods that define the sociological approach to culture from four of the hottest, most up-and-coming scholars in the field. The chapters in "Sociological Critiques of Culture" illustrate distinctively sociological interpretations of cultural phenomena, ranging from images of beauty and conceptions of the body to festivals celebrating comic books and fringe art. Finally, "Culture as Ways of Life" describes and analyzes unique subcultural communities whose significance and mere existence are otherwise easy to miss or misunderstand.

Each of the concise, accessible chapters in this volume reflects TSP's distinctive layout, tone, and style. Sprinkled throughout are short "TSP Tie-Ins," highlighting new and emerging work on the website and in the field. The volume concludes with a Discussion Guide and Group Activities section that challenges readers to draw connections among the chapters, think more deeply and critically about culture and social life, and link to ongoing conversations and interactive posts online.

# introduction

**DOUGLAS HARTMANN AND CHRISTOPHER UGGEN**

When we started, *culture* was kind of a catch-all category—a heading under which we filed all that great, funky, provocative content popping up on the site (and in the field) that didn't quite fit into the more formal and familiar sociological areas like race, gender, or crime. It was a fortuitous decision. Almost as soon as we settled on *culture* as an organizing concept, we suddenly found ourselves with a ton of content on objects and practices—ranging from church rituals and zombies to music festivals, body images, global fashion, and emerging and historic societal trends—that other disciplines and fields didn't have much to say about but our readers reveled in. We became convinced that sociologists were not only best positioned among social scientists to provide commentary and analysis on these intriguing but oft-ignored aspects of contemporary social life but also that this material provided a powerful platform for drawing out key aspects of the uniquely sociological vision of and approach to the study of human life.

Thinking about pulling it together into a single, greatest-hits volume, however, we began to realize that organizing and systematizing it all wasn't going to be easy. Part of the problem was that the organizing scheme we set up in our other volumes (wherein we distinguished core contributions, broader social contexts, and critical theoretical interventions) didn't work so well for this content. We couldn't figure out which pieces fit into which sections: Some seemed like they could fit in almost any place, whereas others didn't appear to have any place at all. Also, perhaps more fundamentally, we began to see that our various contributions and contributors had very different conceptions of what culture was, and they sometimes came from competing orientations to sociology and the study of society. We had something of a multifarious monster on our hands.

To try to make sense of this cacophony of content, we went back to the literature on sociology and culture, itself one of the largest and most vibrant areas of sociological scholarship in recent decades. As we read and discussed key works and ideas, we realized that the subfields that focused on culture in and around sociology were marked by many of the same tensions and confusions we were seeing in our assemblage of texts. Depending on the author or the piece, culture could be a variable in an explanatory model or statistical analysis or it could refer to some distinctive social phenomenon that called for analysis and interpretation all its own. For some, cultural phenomena referred to the more subjective dimensions of social life—ideas, meanings, understandings, ideologies; for others, culture was best conceived as a collection of material objects or social practices. For still others, culture called to mind a distinctive theoretical framework, a unique approach to the study of social life. And for those from a more anthropological or ethnographic tradition, culture functioned as a master concept, much like *society* does in sociology.

We shouldn't have been surprised. The great literary theorist Raymond Williams has called *culture* one of the two or three most complicated words in the English language, and already in the 1950s anthropologists had identified over 100 different meanings and uses of the term. And as we reflected on all of this, we came to realize that what was most exciting and interesting to us was not determining the single best or most useful way to study culture. Rather, we were fascinated by how the whole package of diverse and sometimes competing conceptions of culture and orientations to sociological analysis of it somehow comes together and coheres in this space.

The organizational scheme that resulted reflects this broad, catholic approach. We won't pretend that this volume offers a definitive, all-purpose conception of culture or advocates for one hot new methodological innovation over another. We won't stake out a particular theoretical position about the best way to understand culture's role in social life or relation to social structure. What we can promise, instead, is that each of the sections provides a provocative and useful introduction to all the different kinds of sociological research and writing that falls under the category of *cultural,* the different ways that we study culture, and the unique ways in which the study of culture allows us to think about the social worlds we live in.

## section-by-section organization

*Getting Culture* is organized into three main sections, each of which highlights distinctive aspects of the sociological vision of and approach to the culture concept. "Cultural Sociology" provides a broad sampling of the unique subjects, materials, and methods that constitute the diverse core of culture as it is conceived of by sociologists. The chapters in "Sociological Critiques of Culture" illustrate distinctive, socially grounded interpretations of a range of cultural objects. Finally, "Culture as Ways of Life" describes and analyzes unique subcultural communities as a way to draw out their underlying social structure and broader cultural significance.

## CULTURAL SOCIOLOGY

The diverse chapters in the "Cultural Sociology" section represent some of the distinctive ways sociologists think about culture and connect it to social structure. Kathleen Hull's analysis of the seismic shifts in American public opinion about same-sex marriage is in the tradition of seeing culture as ideas and attitudes that not only reflect social structure but also shape social practices and public policies. Daniel Winchester's chapter takes a much different tack, showing how religious beliefs can be understood as embodied within material icons and collective ritual experiences. In Chapter 3, Sarah Lageson's interview with Jennifer Lena about the formation of identities and networks through musical genres illustrates another distinctive sociological contribution to the study of culture: its collective aspects. These are the things we do and think together, in community and through cultural engagement and consumption. Then Claudio Benzecry's field study of the global fashion industry reminds us of the (often forgotten) organizations, networks, and social processes that come together in the production (and ultimately consumption) of cultural objects and phenomenon.

## SOCIOLOGICAL CRITIQUES OF CULTURE

Another fundamentally sociological insight is that the ways in which the social world is constructed and experienced are extremely varied, context specific, and rarely unproblematic. The "Sociological Critiques" section's unifying theme and contribution are to provide alternative ways of thinking about and viewing culture and its implications in social life. First, Kyle Green brings together two different exchanges with sociologists on the cultural construction and societal stigmatization of specific physical conditions to remind of us how our bodies—those ostensibly material, seemingly invariant, and universal vessels our selves are defined by and housed in—are, in fact, not natural. They are made in ways that have serious and often difficult implications for their inhabitants. The next two chapters provide engaging examples of two of today's most prominent starting points for sociological critique: critical race sociologist C. N. Le's observations and insights into the peculiar, deeply stereotypical ways in which Asian and Asian American beauty is constructed and understood in the United States and around the world today, and Natalie Wilson's feminist take-down of the sexualized and patriarchal images and assumptions built into San Diego's famous Comic-Con, an event and community in which she's lovingly embedded. And then there is the Roundtable exchange convened by cultural sociologist Matt Wray on "that thing in the desert"—the annual Burning Man festival. Without getting lost in the specifics, this exchange illustrates the multitude of ways in which sociologically oriented scholars understand, explain, criticize, and dissect the same cultural thing.

## CULTURE AS WAYS OF LIFE

What makes certain lifestyles and communities distinctive? How and why do people subscribe to different lifeworlds and world views? These questions animate the third section of the book. The first chapter is an interview with Eric Klinenberg about the experience of and increasing attraction to living single. What makes Klinenberg's research so interesting and fundamentally sociological is that he helps us not only understand what it is like to live alone but also to see the broader social forces that make the solo lifestyle possible and appealing across an array of demographics. The next two chapters come out of interviews with ethnographers Colin Jerolmack and Gabriella Coleman. Jerolmack's research on pigeon racing illustrates that unique, sociological ability to find meaning and significance in the most idiosyncratic practices, focusing here on the interplay of human/nonhuman interactions and the importance of deep play as the basis for community. Coleman's studies of Internet activism help bring out the collective dimensions of human experiences that can otherwise seem isolated and isolating, and her emphasis on humor reminds readers of the human side of activities that otherwise seem so rational, serious, and high stakes. The final chapter comes from TSP blogger Nathan Jurgenson and critiques the critiques of online interaction. Part of a long line of sociology concerned with shifting human relationships with technology and media and the fact that the entire TSP project is based on online interaction and publishing, we simply couldn't skip this hot topic.

———

Sociology has long prided itself on being the broadest, most synthetic of the social studies disciplines—the big tent, the queen of the social sciences, the original interdisciplinary discipline. There may be no area that reflects this grand scope and ambition better than research in and on culture. In assembling exemplary selections from this corpus of work, we hope that message will be manifest. The payoff of all these exercises and excursions may be less immediate and concrete than studies of specific social problems or political processes. But seeing culture in the big picture—seeing the different ways in which it can be conceptualized and operationalized, set in relation to social life/social structure—can open our eyes to dimensions and processes of social life whose social significance we otherwise miss, misunderstand, or underestimate.

What is culture? Culture is a lot of things; it is everywhere. Putting this all under a sociological lens helps us figure out what culture is and helps us see society and social life in new ways that go well beyond the literal, material, utilitarian, and commonsense views that so often obscure the real stuff of social life.

As always, we must express our gratitude to the University of Minnesota, W. W. Norton & Company (in particular, the sociology editor, Sasha Levitt, and her predecessor and our early champion, Karl Bakeman), and The Society Pages' graduate student board, several of whom are included as authors in this volume. Evan Stewart is our project's graduate editor. Kyle Green and Stephen Suh were the graduate editors of this volume, and they authored the Discussion Guide and TSP Tie-Ins found throughout. Our associate editor and producer is the incomparable Letta Page.

# changing lenses: exploring dora

**DOUGLAS HARTMANN WITH WING YOUNG HUIE**

The Changing Lenses project is a collaboration and ongoing conversation between The Society Pages' editor in chief Doug Hartmann and award-winning documentary photographer and community activist Wing Young Huie. In this installment, Hartmann had told Huie he'd like to discuss a photo of Huie's choice—the mandate was to choose a photo that captured some aspect of culture. When Huie sent back his photo of a young Minneapolis woman wrapped in a *Dora the Explorer* blanket, Hartmann was initially unsure how to react.

**Wing Young Huie:** Hey Doug, it was great to see your latest post and thoughts about "found sociology" and about the trap of the documentary approach. I wonder

© Wing Young Huie, reprinted with permission.

about [this] in my own work, but try not to think about too much—try to keep my head down (or up) and just keep producing.

Over the years I've come to realize that I'm attracted to photographing the various ways people are mirrored (or not mirrored) culturally. I've never watched any episodes of *Dora the Explorer*, but when I was growing up there weren't any Asian cartoon leading characters, so I related to white characters like Jonny Quest and his father, Race, rather than his brown exotic sidekick, Hadji.

**Doug Hartmann:** When I first looked at your photograph, without seeing your comment, I was kind of puzzled. I loved the image but wasn't quite sure how to place it or what to make of it. Was it supposed to illustrate some general point about diversity? Or something about middle-class life? Then, I thought perhaps it was something about kids and families—because I not only saw a mom and daughter but also started wondering if the mom was supposed to be pregnant. . . .

Once I got past those initial thoughts/impressions, I did notice the Dora blanket, and it definitely did get me thinking about popular culture (as it sounds like was your initial intent), though I was thinking more about kids than race/ethnicity. [When] I finally read your note, it all fell into place. How silly and slow I felt. I mean, I almost always describe my research as being about race and popular culture, and then when you send an image intended to be right in my wheelhouse, I almost don't even notice!

. . . Let me say one specific thing to further the point and conversation: I think it is very difficult (or can be) to situate actual human beings in the context of our mass media and popular culture visually. Like so much of culture and society, it is always there, permeating our thoughts and existence, but often quite difficult to represent. This image obviously overcomes that problem, and I can't wait to see the others you've been taking with a similar theme and sensibility in mind.

**Huie:** I think the meanings of a photo are the least clear when I'm actually in the process of taking it. I was photographing members of Light of Faith and Hope in Jesus Christ, a small storefront church where most, if not all, of the members are Latino. There were a variety of after-the-service-activities that I shot, including a birthday party, a piñata smashing, and a basement buffet, before I saw the girl wrapped up in a cartoon character who really resembled her (as much as a real person can look like an oversimplified caricature of a human being).

It's refreshing to me that you first saw this as just a picture of a family; that you reacted to it perhaps as a father rather than a professional sociologist. Sometimes I worry that reading photos through the prism of culture and identity, as is my wont, may blind a person to everyday humanness.

As we continue to explore the nexus of our respective fields, I wonder how much of what I do focuses on the specific, while sociology is concerned with the general. I am reminded of something Diane Arbus said: "It was my teacher, Lisette Model, who finally made it clear to me that the more specific you are, the more general it'll be."

**Hartmann:** First, I think I understand and appreciate what you mean when you say that the meanings of a photograph are the "least clear" when you are actually taking a picture. That point reminds me that so many of the meanings and implications we derive and project onto cultural objects like your photographs are derived not just from the image but from what each of us brings to those images and the conversations and exchanges that they occasion and prompt. That's one of the fun, creative aspects of our whole project, in fact.

But I'd also like to point out—wearing my sociology hat—that when you sketch out the context within which a particular shot is taken . . . it really helps shape and determine how and what I will think about a particular image, what meanings and implications I see in it, impart to it, or develop from it.

Sociologists think about the relationship between the specific, the general, and the universal all the time. Something unique can stand in for a larger concept. I am also very interested to hear that you think so much about the relationship between the specific and the general, the particular, and the more universal—and these especially in the context of what you call "everyday humanness." One analytic concept this calls to mind is *representation* or *representativeness,* how something unique or particular can and necessarily does stand in for a larger concept, category, or group. Is this what you mean by "the prism of culture"? On this note, I'm less than certain, actually, about what you mean by your question about whether the "cartoon landscape is catching up to real cultural representation"? . . . I guess I'm not sure what is "real," independent from our ability to represent it in some way and make sense of that representation with respect to other, more general categories and experiences. . . .

**Huie:** Not only are the meanings least clear the moment when I press the shutter, I'm not sure if the resulting image ever becomes clarified. In a way, the more meanings that are possible, the more successful the photo is in my mind. I'm often surprised at someone's interpretation, and each layer of interpretation affects how I look at it.

When I started photography over 35 years ago, I had this kind of pure notion that there shouldn't be any words or even titles accompanying a photo—the image should stand on its own. But over the years, I've added more and more text and context, sometimes I think too much. [It might rob] the viewers of their own interpretation. Perhaps that shift comes from an increasing desire to inform, rather than this idea of photography for photography's sake.

Since I wasn't represented in popular culture, I became what I saw. I forgot what I looked like. I guess what I mean by "prism of culture" is that I often think about the cultural implications of a photo. This may have to do with the fact that, when I was growing up, there seemed to be few people in popular culture who looked like me—just kung fu characters and Connie Chung. Since I wasn't "represented," I became what I saw and forgot what I looked like.

I was always the only Asian student in my school, from kindergarten until senior high when another Asian kid appeared at Duluth Central High School. I ended up avoiding this kid. It took me a long time to realize—not until I was working on my "Looking for Asian America: An Ethnocentric Tour"—[to start] thinking about why I would avoid someone who looked like me.

In my mind, growing up, I thought I was like everyone else. It's not like you grow up with a mirror in front of you. Popular culture becomes your mirror. And popular culture is a distorted mirror. . . .

The World of Disney, I'm sure, had a lot to do in shaping my world and my view of myself. But, as I mentioned, there were few Asian cartoon characters, and I wonder if even the nonhuman characters such as Bugs Bunny, were made with a white, male, Christian point of view for a white, male, Christian audience. And how long did it take to finally have a major cartoon character like Dora that reflected America's now-minority-but-eventual-majority Latino population?

# cultural sociology: how we think and what we do

# same sex,
# different attitudes

**KATHLEEN E. HULL**

Ten short years ago, same-sex marriage produced deep divisions within American society. The majority of Americans opposed granting legal recognition to gay and lesbian couples, and politicians seemed to play tug-of-war with the issue as it suited their needs. In 2003, Massachusetts became the first state to grant marriage licenses to same-sex couples when its high court ruled that withholding marriage recognition violated the state's constitution. In the meantime, in his 2004 State of the Union address, President George W. Bush called for an amendment to the federal constitution to block same-sex marriages nationwide. Gavin Newsom, then the mayor of San Francisco, responded a month later by opening marriage to same-sex couples at San Francisco City Hall. It was a short-lived policy, ultimately shut down by the courts, but it drew frenzied media attention; images of two brides or two grooms tying the knot graced TV screens and newspapers' front pages, no longer rhetoric but reality.

By the November 2004 general election, 11 states voted on—and, ultimately, for—ballot measures to amend their state constitutions to ban same-sex marriages. Some even argued that those ballot measures played a decisive role in Bush's reelection; at a minimum, the initiatives represented a clear right-wing strategy to get socially conservative voters to the polls in a tight election year. In a happy coincidence for the incumbent, those who voted for same-sex marriage bans generally also took the time to vote for the Republican presidential candidate.

Now, in 2014, things look quite different. President Barack Obama publicly declared his support for same-sex marriage in the midst of his 2012 reelection campaign, and less than a year later, the U.S. Supreme Court ruled a section of the federal Defense of Marriage Act (DOMA) unconstitutional. The move opened the door for federal recognition of the same-sex marriages that had been performed in "legal" states. Some Republican strategists now think the issue is a "loser" for their party as national polls have started to show majority support for legal same-sex marriage. Although opinion differs dramatically by region, those young and middle-aged, middle-class white voters Republicans could long count on are becoming more liberal on the marriage issue, and political operatives are all too aware that a firm stand against marriage equality might siphon off once-staunch, party-line voters.

When an issue seemingly inspired such passion and division just a decade ago, how could it so quickly have become an election day loser?

First, a look at the numbers. The figure below shows Gallup poll results on same-sex marriage going back to 1996, the year that Congress passed DOMA. The poll asked: "Do you think marriages between same-sex couples should or should not be recognized by the law as valid, with the same rights as traditional marriages?" Between 1996 and July

Americans' Views on Legal Same-Sex Marriage

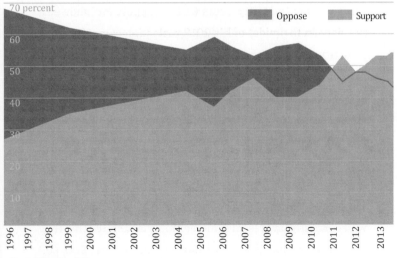

Source: Gallup News Poll
Graphic created for TheSocietyPages.org by Suzy McElrath

2013, the proportion of respondents who said same-sex marriages should be valid rose from 27 percent to 54 percent. The proportion saying such marriages should *not* be valid declined from 68 percent to 43 percent. (A small proportion of respondents, never exceeding 5 percent, offered no opinion on the issue.) Other polls, worded differently, have yielded similar results. For example, Pew Research Center asks: "Do you strongly favor, favor, oppose, or strongly oppose allowing gays and lesbians to marry legally?" In 2003, the Pew question yielded 34 percent in favor and 56 percent opposed to same-sex marriage; by 2013, 49 percent of Americans were in favor and 44 percent opposed. A 2013 *Washington Post/ABC News Poll* asking, "Do you think it should be legal or illegal for gay and lesbian couples to get married?" showed a 58–36 percent divide, with the majority preferring "legal."

Attitude change that occurs this quickly and on this scale cannot be explained in the usual ways. It's not a case of older people with more conservative beliefs dying out and being replaced by younger, more liberal generations (what social scientists refer to as a cohort replacement effect). Rather, this kind of rapid shift suggests some individuals are changing their minds on the issue. Indeed, a recent Pew Research Center report noted that more than a quarter of Americans who currently favor legal same-sex marriage stated that they had changed their view on this issue. Historical Pew poll numbers back this up: Support for same-sex marriage rose *within* every age cohort between 2003 and 2013, although age is still a good predictor of views on this issue. For example, support for same-sex marriage among the so-called Silent Generation (those born between 1928 and 1945) rose from only 17 percent in 2003 to 31 percent in 2013, while support among millennials (those born after 1980) increased from 51 percent to 70 percent. Acceptance of same-sex marriage is rising at roughly the same rate across generations, but the starting point—those first poll results—is much lower for each previous generation.

So if it's not just a cohort replacement, what has caused this large-scale shift? Several different factors likely contributed. In the March 2013 Pew poll, respondents who said they had changed their minds were also asked why. About a third stated that it had come through knowing someone who was gay, and a quarter attributed the change to getting older, becoming more open, and thinking about the issue more. Smaller proportions cited the prevalence and seeming inevitability of same-sex marriage, the idea that everyone should have freedom of choice without government interference, or a general belief in equal rights.

Beyond these self-reported reasons, at least two other factors have probably contributed to changing views. One is the growing cultural visibility of same-sex relationships and families headed by same-sex couples. Two decades ago, gay and lesbian characters were relatively rare on TV shows and in movies; when comedian Ellen DeGeneres and her sitcom alter ego came out in 1997, it was a major news event. Some TV stations refused to air the coming-out episode of her show. Today, films like *Brokeback Mountain* can be nominated for Best Picture Oscars, and characters like same-sex couple Cam and Mitchell on the TV comedy *Modern Family* enjoy more plotline attention for their parenting foibles than their sexual orientation. Cultural visibility like this familiarizes people, and for some individuals, that increased familiarity is enough to soften opposition to homosexuality and gay rights.

A second factor that has likely contributed to declining opposition to same-sex marriage is the fact that such marriages are now legal in several U.S. states and in many countries. At the time of this writing, 35 states and the District of Columbia, along with 18 countries outside the United States, recognize same-sex marriage. Not only has the relatively rapid spread of legal same-sex marriage created a sense of inevitability (as noted by some respondents in the 2013 Pew poll) but it also casts doubt on some of the arguments against legal recognition. As more jurisdictions institute legal same-sex marriage and there's no subsequent clear evidence of harmful outcomes, the direst predictions about marriage

## State Same-Sex Marriage Laws

**Provisions Allowing Same-Sex Marriage**

- No Provisions
- Voter Approved Ballot Measure
- Judicial Decision
- Legislative Action

Source: National Council of State Legislatures
Graphic created for TheSocietyPages.org by Suzy McElrath

equality's negative effects on "traditional" marriages and children lose credibility.

Changing attitudes about same-sex marriage are occurring in the broader context of changing beliefs about the moral acceptability of homosexuality and other sex-related behaviors. On most of these issues, the general trend has been toward greater acceptance. In Gallup's annual "Values and Beliefs" poll, the proportion of Americans saying that gay and lesbian relations are morally acceptable climbed from 40 percent in 2001 to 59 percent in 2013, the largest percentage-point change for any of the 20 issues covered by the survey. (By way of comparison, the proportion saying having a baby outside of marriage was morally acceptable rose from 45 percent to 60 percent, and acceptance of sex between an unmarried man and unmarried woman went from 53 percent to 63 percent.) Views on the moral status of homosexual conduct almost certainly influence attitudes toward same-sex marriage.

In fact, numerous studies have established that being female, younger, and more highly educated are all associated with greater acceptance of homosexuality and support for same-sex marriage. Those who attend religious services regularly, identify as Republican, and live outside cities generally have less tolerant views. In addition, people who personally know gay men, lesbians, or bisexuals are more accepting; people who believe homosexuality is a choice are less so.

In a recent analysis of General Social Survey data from 1988 through 2010, sociologist Dawn Michelle Baunach found that only four characteristics were significant predictors of level of support for same-sex marriage across all survey years: religious attendance, political affiliation, education, and gender. Back in 1988, support for same-sex marriage was mostly limited to highly educated urbanites who were not religious conservatives. By 2010, opposition to same-sex marriage had become localized to older Americans, Southerners, African Americans, evangelical Protestants, and Republicans. Baunach concluded that most of the change in same-sex marriage attitudes was due to a general cultural shift that transcended demographic categories rather than to changes in the composition of the population or the strength of the influence of certain characteristics on people's views.

As Americans' views of same-sex marriage are shifting, opponents and advocates of legal same-sex marriage continually adjust their legal and political strategies. Over the last couple of decades, opponents of same-sex marriage have moved away from strategies that vilify gays and lesbians as immoral and toward arguments emphasizing a concern for children and religious freedom. This shift was probably motivated in part by the recognition that a declining proportion of Americans had moral objections to homosexuality per se. On the other side, proponents of legal same-sex marriage are shifting away from the language of rights and highlighting the universality of love and equal legal protection of all families. Post mortem political research conducted after votes on same-sex ballot measures found the simple message that loving relationships and families of all kinds deserve social support resonated with average voters. Rights-based arguments mostly fell flat.

In ways that may surprise many, the marriage issue has proven controversial even within lesbian, gay, bisexual, and transgender (LGBT) communities. Queer critics argue that marriage is a mechanism of social and sexual control, thus antithetical to the founding principles of gay liberation. LGBT feminists express concern that same-sex marriage cannot be disentangled from the patriarchal roots of the institution of marriage itself. Other LGBT skeptics question whether marriage has been the right area of focus for the gay rights movement, given that basic LGBT antidiscrimination protections are still paltry and that marriage may benefit only a small segment of the community (namely, middle-class lesbians and gay men who desire social assimilation). But in interview research that Timothy Ortyl and I conducted with LGBT people in the Minneapolis–St. Paul area, we found little support for the idea that same-sex marriage is mainly important to more privileged members of this population. And U.S. Census data on same-sex couples indicate that those couples raising children (who might reap significant practical benefits from access to marriage) are actually disproportionately lower-income people of color, not upper-middle-class whites intent on assimilating into the American nuclear family ideal.

And it's far from clear that the "traditional" nuclear family holds a prominent place in the American cultural imagination today. The debates over same-sex marriage have unfolded alongside rapid change in Americans' general beliefs and practices concerning marriage and family formation. With almost half of all first marriages ending in divorce and nearly half of all children being born to unmarried parents, the meanings and practices of marriage and family evolve toward greater diversity. Most Americans still desire marriage, but many no longer view it as essential to a happy life. Further, the ideal of a single marriage as a lifelong commitment bumps up against the realities of longer lifespans and the declining stigma of divorce.

A recent study by sociologist Brian Powell and colleagues affirmed that Americans' definitions of family were broadening at a rapid pace. Between 2003 and 2006, the proportion who held the most restrictive definitions of *family* (definitions that generally included only married, heterosexual couples with children) fell from 45 percent to 38 percent. Those with the broadest definitions, including same-sex and heterosexual couples with or without children, married or unmarried, rose from 25 percent to 32 percent. These are large changes, given the short time period. A follow-up survey in 2010 found a further broadening in definitions of family.

Taken together, the evolution of Americans' attitudes about same-sex marriage has not one but several underlying causes. As more gays and lesbians come out to friends and family, more people feel a personal connection to the issue. The passage of time gives people a chance to get used to the idea of same-sex marriage. And with more jurisdictions implementing legal same-sex marriage, some people have come to see its spread as inevitable. Others have noted that the sky has not fallen on those trailblazing states and countries—the consequences some predicted simply haven't come to pass. True, some of the change is due to cohort replacement, but this accounts for only a small proportion of the overall change. Increasing cultural visibility and declining moral disapproval of homosexuality have real, if difficult to measure, effects. Political advocates of same-sex marriage, more effective and research-based, may also account for some of the change. Most broadly, changes in the nature of marriage and family—changes that touch virtually all Americans directly or indirectly—cause many of us to rethink our personal definitions of marriage and family, as well as the purposes and effectiveness of laws and policies that favor some definitions over others.

## RECOMMENDED READING

Dawn Michelle Baunach. 2012. "Changing Same-Sex Marriage Attitudes in America from 1988 through 2010." *Public Opinion Quarterly* 76(2): 364–378. An analysis of General Social Survey data identifying key predictors of views on same-sex marriage, noting that demographic shifts explain little of the change.

Mary Bernstein and Verta Taylor, editors. 2013. *The Marrying Kind? Debating Same-Sex Marriage within the Lesbian and Gay Movement.* Minneapolis: University of Minnesota Press. A collection of papers examining debates within LGBT communities on the marriage question.

Andrew Cherlin. 2009. *The Marriage-Go-Round: The State of Marriage and Family in America Today.* New York: Knopf. An examination of contemporary views and practices related to marriage and family, underlining the high instability in U.S. families resulting from Americans' contradictory impulses toward marital commitment and individual freedom.

Pew Research Center. 2013. *Growing Support for Gay Marriage: Changed Minds and Changing Demographics.* Washington, DC: Pew. A summary report of recent attitude trends, including acceptance of same-sex marriage, homosexuality, and same-sex parenting.

Brian Powell, Catherine Bolzendahl, Claudia Geist, and Lala Carr Steelman. 2010. *Counted Out: Same-Sex Relations and Americans' Definitions of Family.* New York: Russell Sage Foundation. A survey-based exploration of Americans' evolving definitions of family, identifying trends toward broader definitions.

# the feel of faith

**DANIEL WINCHESTER**

2

"So, what is it they believe?" As a sociologist of religion, I'm used to getting some variant of this question when colleagues, students, or curious friends want me to describe a religious community I happen to be studying. And, as a cultural sociologist, I'm sympathetic to this line of questioning. Cultural scholars of religion have long argued that in order to fully understand how religion shapes human behavior, we need to pay attention to and take seriously the powerful role that religious meanings play in the lives of adherents. Religious symbols, as the famous anthropologist Clifford Geertz noted, instill some of the fundamental "moods and motivations" by which worshipers experience and act in the world. What better way to understand the power of such meanings than to learn about their beliefs—what they believe about God, the nature of the universe, the purpose and meaning of life?

Yet, as sympathetic as I am to the "What do they believe?" question, it can also limit our understanding of religious meaning and experience. The question presumes that once we know the basic ideas or concepts behind a religious individual or community's most important symbols, we've gotten to know something essential about them. In this view, what it means to "be religious," either at the individual or group level, is acceptance of and adherence to a set of abstract doctrines—that there is no God but Allah and that Muhammad is his messenger, for example, or that Jesus Christ is the son of God and born of a virgin.

Such beliefs are certainly central to any thorough understanding of a religious individual, community, or tradition, but focusing too heavily on these aspects can also give us a disembodied, dematerialized, and even asocial understanding of religious meaning and experience. This is because to be religious isn't only about accepting specific doctrines. It is also about entering into a specific kind of sensory environment, one that materially engages and organizes individual and collective bodies in particular ways. It is to feel the wooden pews, prayer rugs, or carpeted floors under your backside; to taste the bread at communion or the dates at the end of the day's fast; to see the magnificence of the massive arches and stained glass windows at St. Paul's Cathedral or the simplicity of a prayer circle at a Quaker meeting; to hear the sounds of hymnals, scriptural recitations, or ecstatic worship. Taking seriously these embodied and material

© Daniel Winchester, reprinted with permission.

aspects of religious life allows us to begin to understand that when someone says, "I believe that Jesus Christ is Lord" or that "There is no God but Allah and Muhammad was his messenger" or "The Goddess resides within each of us," what we are hearing is only the tip of a much vaster and deeper structure of cultural meaning and experience. Submerged beneath explicit statements of belief are a lifetime's worth of bodily engagements with the literal "stuff" of religious life—the familiar feel of hands folded and head bowed in evening prayers, the taste of dates after breaking the Ramadan fast with family, the look in a favorite saint's eyes during a time of crisis, the sounds of chanting during a pilgrimage.

What I'm arguing here is that while it is perfectly reasonable and necessary to ask what religious people believe, to more fully understand the cultural dimensions of religious life, we also need to complement this emphasis on belief with a focus on the sensual and material aspects of religious practice. In other words, we need to appreciate the underlying aesthetic dimensions of religious culture—the literal *feel* of the faith.

Religion, of course, is only one area of social life where cultural sociologists do their research. But a focus on the aesthetics of religious culture is relevant for any researcher interested in how particular cultural meanings become important—even sacred—for different social groups. Nationalist symbols like the American flag, for example, generate meanings not only from ideas about patriotism and national myths but also from sensory engagements within concrete social communities. Growing up in the United States, many of us were socialized into patriotic beliefs by pledging our allegiance, not an abstract belief but a collective practice that involved complex social relationships between material locales and objects (school desks, chairs, white stars and red and white stripes), bodily comportments that engaged the senses (standing up, eyes on the flag, with hand over heart), and, of course, other people (students, teachers, fellow citizens). Religion, then, is just one very interesting social microcosm in which to explore what social theorist Raymond Williams termed the *structures of feeling* undergirding cultural life as a whole.

## seeing and believing

For my own part, the importance of the aesthetic side of religious culture became very apparent when I began a recent research project on Eastern Orthodox Christianity in the contemporary United States. While not as widely known as Protestantism and Catholicism in the United States, the Eastern Orthodox Church is actually the second largest Christian body in the world today, with 225 to 300 million adherents worldwide (about 1.2 million in the United States). Walk into a Russian, Greek, Serbian, Syrian, or any of the other 16 churches that make up the Orthodox Christian communion on a given Sunday morning, and you'll be exposed to a vibrant religious culture that extends back to the founding first century of the Christian faith.

Bodily engagements with material objects and artifacts are essential to this tradition. During rites, incense fills your nostrils, the chanting of priests and deacons performing the Divine Liturgy ring in your ears and, perhaps most striking, the faces of saints, the Virgin Mary (or *Theotokos*, as the Orthodox often call her, using the Greek for "God-bearer"), and Jesus Christ (the religion's savior and son of God) seem

© Daniel Winchester, reprinted with permission.

to stare from all corners of the church. Painted on flat wooden panels with extraordinary color and detail, the holy iconography of the Eastern Orthodox tradition adorns the walls and ceiling of the church. Both abundant and aesthetically intricate, the icons are impossible to ignore.

For Orthodox Christians, icons are much more than decoration. They are said to literally make present holy figures. Those who interact with icons are allowed tangible access to an otherwise invisible relationship with the figure portrayed in the image. The subject of the icon is also, in some sense, at one with the icon; it has a spiritual presence beyond but also within the material object. In common Orthodox parlance, these icons are "windows onto heaven," and they extend the presence of holy persons into devotees' everyday lives.

On one hand, we could simply say that the Eastern Orthodox believe that icons make holy figures literally present to the faithful. This would certainly be true. On the other hand, sticking strictly to the language of belief, while at least giving attention to these material objects, still misses how icons are active partners in the creation and maintenance of belief. Orthodox Christians don't just believe things *about* icons, they believe *through* them—they pray with them in times of contemplation, they kiss them in moments of gratitude, they venerate them as a matter of admiration and respect, they implore them in times of frustration and despair. Icons are not mere placeholders for already existing religious beliefs.

They are aesthetic mediators of social relationships and cultural meaning. They are matter that matters.

## a cloud of witnesses

"Since we are surrounded by so great a cloud of witnesses, let us lay aside every earthly care and . . . run with perseverance the race that is set before us, looking to Jesus, the author and finisher of our faith" (Hebrews 12:1–2).

Émile Durkheim, one of the founding fathers of the sociology of religion, noted long ago that religious objects often serve as a symbolic representation of the larger community. They help a group imagine and commemorate itself as a collective. Contemporary scholar of religious images David Morgan elaborates that material images like icons create "visual situations in which viewers assume a position within a set of relations."

For Eastern Orthodox communities, icons are a constant reminder that humans are positioned in a set of social relations that span the divides between life and death, heaven and earth. Icons represent a great cloud of witnesses who commune with the faithful. Even within the entrance to the church (the narthex), icons surround you. They often depict Christ, the Holy Trinity, Mary, and important saints such as John the Baptist and Saint John Chrysostom. The faithful stop to

© Daniel Winchester, reprinted with permission.

venerate these icons, which consists of looking the depicted
figure in the eyes, crossing one's self, bowing before the
revered figure, and then kissing and sometimes lightly touch-
ing the icon (usually near where the hands or feet of the holy
figure are depicted).

This cycle of crossing, bowing, and kissing continues as
church members enter the main hall (the nave). Here, an
icon depicting the patron saint of the church often stands
at the entrance. This icon is venerated first, followed by an

icon of Christ and then other saints depicted near the iconostasis (a veritable wall of iconography that separates the nave, where lay persons worship, from the sanctuary and the tabernacle, areas where the Eucharist—the mixture of bread and wine believed to be the body and blood of Christ—is located and where only priests are allowed until the taking of communion at the end of the liturgy). Above the tabernacle hangs a crucifix—a depiction of Christ on the cross, an image that shows the faithful their savior dying for their sins. Higher still, an even larger depiction of Christ inside the church's dome looks down upon all who have congregated there.

During the liturgy itself, the icons also feature prominently. Several times during the two-hour ritual, which includes the collective singing of hymns, reading of biblical scriptures, prayers, and communion, icons are carried by clergy, and the faithful again venerate the saints as they pass by.

For newcomers, the physical adoration of these objects may seem strange. The Orthodox faithful, who have seen an influx of inquirers and even a sizable number of converts to their churches in recent years, understand. "I know that it's probably very strange for them at first," a woman named Marjorie told me one Sunday at coffee hour after the liturgy, "seeing all of these pictures of these strange-looking people, and all of us Orthodox kissing them and crossing ourselves in front of them. But I take it as my job to make it un-strange for them. I just say, 'I want to introduce you to some of my dear friends.'"

Being introduced to a saint or other holy figure through an icon is, in fact, a way in which people are brought into this larger church community. Established Orthodox members often give icons to new members as gifts, selecting a saint with whom the new worshiper might share some kind of affinity. Peter, a lifelong member of an Orthodox church in Saint Paul, Minnesota, explains:

> I've been fortunate enough to be a sponsor for several of the new members of our church. And, with a lot of the new converts, I try to give them or lead them to icons that they might feel a connection with. You know, like I've given icons of Christ the teacher and Saint John Chrysostom to people who are educators, or icons of Mary or Joseph to people I know are really doting and fretful parents—God knows, there are plenty of those! Or, you know, maybe something even a bit more personal if the person has confided in me that they struggle with a particular problem in their life, because we all do. Because the amazing thing about the saints is that they were people, just like us. They weren't perfect. In fact, many of them started out their lives as really damaged, sinful people. So they have their human flaws and foibles, just like we do. But, through their icons, they also let us see that, if you turn toward God and the church, you can overcome your sins.

In and through the exchange of icons, people like Marjorie and Peter encourage new members to look at the icon and see

© Daniel Winchester, reprinted with permission.

not a strange picture of a long-dead saint but a fellow community member, a friend—someone kind of like themselves. Further, in and through the circulation of icons, in liturgical ritual and as sacred gifts, the cloud of witnesses manifests itself in collective practice.

## taking the virgin mary for a drive

Icons not only fill the churches of Eastern Orthodox Christians. Their portability allows the saints to tag along with worshipers into the seemingly mundane spaces of everyday life: homes, workplaces, and even cars.

At home, Orthodox Christians invariably keep what is called an icon corner, usually a small shelf or table placed in the east corner of a room. These spaces have at least one icon of Jesus and the Theotokos, popular saints, and favored saints of the individual and his or her family members. Worshipers go to the icon corner to offer their daily prayers and devotions, whether in the morning, evening, or both. As a man named Alex told me: "I look over at my icon corner and see that I'm never really alone, that there is this larger community around me all the time, praying along with me and encouraging me to keep going along the path I've taken."

Icons, in other words, act as material mediators of religious community. Their presence outside the church space allows even seemingly individual prayers to be experienced as collective.

The aesthetic dimensions of icons also simply demand attention. To put it bluntly, icons look weird to modern eyes, let alone to the nonreligious. In most of our interactions with artwork, for example, we are used to viewing the images with a linear perspective: figures that are farther away are depicted as smaller, giving the viewer the illusion of a naturalistic, three-dimensional image. More geometrically, in most of the art of the past 700 years or so, parallel lines usually converge at what is called a vanishing point, which gives a sense of distance. Icons, however, reverse this perspective, in effect closing distance between religious worshipers and their saints. In traditional Orthodox iconography, figures are enlarged as they go into the distance, diverging against the horizon. The vanishing point is, instead, outside the painting, right where the viewer stands. The effect is an expanding and unfolding toward the viewer.

Moreover, the holy figures are depicted with disproportionately large eyes and ears and small noses and mouths. These features have theological significance, to be sure, but they have profound sensory effects as well. The combination of the large eyes and the inverted perspective creates the illusion that the icon is looking back at you. For worshipers, this is a materialized invitation to greater piety and concentration. As a woman named Kim told me, showing me one of her favorite icons of the Virgin Mary:

> One of the things that—and I'm sure you've noticed this too—
> one of the first things that people notice about icons are
> the eyes. They're usually very big, very round, and it can even
> look distorted and off-putting at first. . . . I think that they are
> there to draw your own eyes to them. . . . Like, with this icon of
> Mary, I focus my eyes on hers, and I feel like she focuses hers
> on mine, and I feel like that keeps the rest of me—my brain
> and my heart—focused where it should be while I'm praying,
> on God. Because where the eyes go, the rest of you will follow.

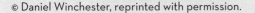
© Daniel Winchester, reprinted with permission.

While icons are an established part of most every Orthodox home, some saints are not content with being home-
bodies. In my research, I regularly witnessed Orthodox
Christians taking an icon or two to work. "Keeping a Christian mind-set is difficult to do on your own," said Charles, a
finance executive in downtown Minneapolis, Minnesota.
One morning I asked Charles about an icon of Christ on his
office wall. He smiled, stood up, and walked me out of his

office. He closed the door behind us. Then, almost immediately, he opened the door and led me back in:

> My wife gave me that after we joined the church together. And I put it here because it is the first thing that I walk past every day when I come into this room, and even if I don't look at Him, I know that He is always watching me. . . . In my business, as I'm sure you probably know from the news right now, people can be tempted to do some pretty unscrupulous things. And that [he points to the icon, for emphasis] is there to remind me of who I'm really called to be like. Because, at the end of the line, I'm not going to be judged on how much money I make for my clients—or for myself, for that matter— but on if I've lived a Christ-like life.

In addition to home and work spaces, smaller, travel-size icons also allow Christ, Mary, and the saints to go on long trips and daily commutes. Showing me a small, book-like icon (a diptych) of Christ and the Theotokos, Hannah told me that she hung an almost identical version from her car's rearview mirror, "I keep this icon in my car because I tend to get very impatient and angry when I drive," she told me, "so my daughter and husband gave me this to help." Examining the detail of the small piece, I asked if it worked. "Well, sometimes," she said laughing, "but sometimes not at all. But it does always remind me to ask for forgiveness right after [laughs]. . . . It's so bad, but I've probably asked Jesus and the

Theotokos for forgiveness in that car more often than I have in a confessional!"

"The saints," one Orthodox priest relayed to me, "are with us everywhere." Now I was seeing how true his words were. Through icons, the saints can be—and regularly are—taken just about anywhere. In taking up icons for their own everyday purposes, the faithful also submit themselves to meaningful forms of icon-mediated bodily discipline. When Charles, for example, placed his icon of Christ in his office, he was submitting not only his gaze but, ideally, all his daily

© Daniel Winchester, reprinted with permission.

actions to the scrutiny of God. Engaging the eyes of the icon, as Kim so aptly put it, was also a matter of disciplining the body, mind, and heart.

The role of icons in the lives of Eastern Orthodox Christians demonstrates just one way aesthetic culture matters in the production and experience of religious meaning. If religion, as scholar Robert Orsi, puts it, is in large part a practice of making the invisible visible, then belief statements alone just won't get the job done. Leaps of faith are real but usually not blind. In most religions, people also seek a felt connection with a sacred reality: The supernatural needs to somehow be made empirical, available to be seen, heard, smelled, tasted, and touched. Aesthetic culture, the embodied and material dimensions of religious life, is the often overlooked domain in which this happens.

## RECOMMENDED READING

Jeffrey C. Alexander, D. Bartmanski, and B. Giesen. 2011. *Iconic Power: Materiality and Meaning in Social Life*. New York: Palgrave Macmillan. A recent collection on the cultural power of icons, religious and secular, in shaping contemporary social life.

Omar M. McRoberts. 2004. "Beyond *Mysterium Tremendum*: Thoughts toward an Aesthetic Study of Religious Experience."

*The Annals of the American Academy of Political and Social Science* 595: 190–203. An acclaimed ethnographer of urban religion ponders how sociology can better understand religious experience through a focus on the aesthetics of worship.

David Morgan. 2012. *The Embodied Eye: Religious Visual Culture and the Social Life of Feeling*. Berkeley: University of California Press. Demonstrates how religious ways of seeing are profoundly embodied social practices that vary across religious communities and traditions.

Robert Orsi. 1996. *Thank You, St. Jude: Women's Devotion to the Patron Saint of Hopeless Causes*. New Haven, CT, and London: Yale University Press. Studies the important role one saint, Jude Thaddeus, has played in the lives of countless American Catholic women.

Geneviève Zubrzycki. 2013. "Aesthetic Revolt and the Remaking of National Identity in Québec, 1960–1969." *Theory and Society* 42: 423–475. A cultural sociologist of religion and nationalism examines how icons of and rituals surrounding Saint John the Baptist have shaped French-speaking Canadians' national identity.

# music and the quest for a tribe with jennifer c. lena

**SARAH LAGESON**

I n her book *Banding Together*, Jennifer Lena introduces readers to a typology of over 60 popular music genres, from bluegrass to rap to South Texas polka. While most musical histories focus on the creativity of individual performers, Lena emphasizes how *communities* matter more than individual musicians. She asks why some music styles gain mass popularity whereas others thrive in small niches. In exploring this question, Lena shows that all musical genres move through similar trajectories; readers can dig into the cultural language and evolution of popular music through the obstacles creative people share.

According to Lena, the dominant approach to understanding music history is focused on "heroic stories—accidents, serendipity, or tragic events. You know, these singular personalities and events that are responsible for the direction that the [music] community takes. So, just to name one example of many, if Yoko Ono hadn't broken up the Beatles." A sociologist, on the other hand, recognizes that though the Ono–Beatles saga is compelling, it treats the Beatles' rise and breakup—even John Lennon's death—as if they had taken place outside of history. With Lena's approach, every single artist and fan exists in a community and a context. Understanding that can help reveal commonalities across musical styles and fan niches.

Lena's study tries to "get to the heart of what it means to think about music as a community, a participatory kind of activity. And across these different styles of communities, across different styles of music, what different things were held in common, what different features were shared across cases." Essential to this study is a sociological definition of *genre*, which is different from the popular use of the term. Lena defines a musical genre as "a system of orientations, expectations and conventions that bind together industry performers, critics, and fans in making what they identify as a distinctive sort of music." She told me she has three distinct reasons for using this definition:

> The first is, the definition is supposed to show you that genres are subject to debate. That people have active conversations about what should count as a style of music no matter what the style of music is. And so any sociologist who wants to

understand how music communities work has to incorporate into their very definition the fact that people will dispute who belongs in the group.

The second thing that I want you to hear in the definition is that there are many different kinds of people and organizations that are involved in making genres. And this is, again, one of the places where I think biographies and autobiographies, musical histories, tend to be more narrowly focused than I am. They tend to look at just the creative people or sometimes the fans. But, of course, a music community doesn't work if there aren't record stores that sell the records and reviewers who review the records and media that do stories on the scene or the people involved. So, I think about a much broader group of people as being involved in musical genres than maybe you might find in a music history.

The final thing that I want you to pay attention to in the definition of genre is that I am not focused on a particular style, that the definition of genre is supposed to be a sociological definition, not a musicological definition. So, let me just quickly contrast those: A musicological definition is something like "jazz as a genre" or "rap as a genre." What I'm actually trying to say is that there are styles of community across musical styles and those things are genres. So, I redefine genre as a type of community.

These community-generated genres move through specific historical trajectories (a sequence or array of things over time and/or space) as they develop. In the case of bands and their fans, Lena is interested in the trajectories of four music genres, or four simple types of community structures:

First we start with the kind of prototypical garage band; I call them *avant-garde genres*. These are small communities where people are usually not even thinking about themselves as making music. Sometimes they think they're just hanging out with their friends after school and there happen to be instruments around. Sometimes they think they're doing political action and there's musical accompaniment.

From time to time, there's enough momentum in the group or enough aspiration to make music that they transform into the second genre form, something I call *scene-based music*. And we know a lot about this; in fact, most people have probably participated in a music scene in their life. This is music you'd find in your community: local bands that play at local clubs and involve people that you went to high school with. Most of them sort of wither and die without people outside the community even knowing that they exist. But from time to time there are sponsors who come in from the outside— usually journalists or record label executives, A&R executives, people who are talent scouts—who come along and decide that the music from this community deserves to be more popular.

If a community makes that transition and becomes pop music, then they've entered what I call the third genre form, *industry-based music*. And this is pop music in all its glory; it's globally distributed, and you can buy the outfit to look like you fit into the community at the mall, and there's lingo and there are *Time* magazine articles about it—it's pop music.

Pop music is a cyclical phenomenon, and it fades from attention. Every so often there's something that sticks around, but for the most part, pop music withers and dies. Yet, in some cases there's a fourth community that emerges. I call them *traditionalists*. These folks form a community around preserving the music. They're not actually interested in preserving the pop music in that style, but the earlier form, the scene-based music. And so these folks are usually academics, journalists, some of the surviving performers from that earlier period.

These four genre forms can be applied to a multitude of specific American musical types that all share a sequence from small to large to preservationists. Lena cites many examples, including bebop jazz in the 1950s and country music starting in the 1930s. About rap music in the 1970s, she says:

Rap music starts in Brooklyn and the South Bronx in the '70s with a bunch of teenagers who are basically throwing house parties. They're really playing what we would call disco and R&B music now, and they decide that they want to make a new kind of music that basically takes out the choruses and all of the parts of the song that have lyrics and focus just on those instrumental breaks between verses of the song. So they figure out a technological way to extend that break, that instrumental part. And in so doing they create a new style of music that we now call rap.

As soon as they start playing it in the local clubs and there are small record labels that are recording it, then we have a scene-based genre. Very soon after that we get the first set of recordings from Rick Rubin and the Def Jam label, and we begin to have rap as pop music in the form of the Beastie Boys and Run–D.M.C. And now, of course, there's a huge industry of preservationists, these traditionalist genre people who are (well, like myself) writing books about it, reissuing albums, doing concert tours.

Tracing these musical trajectories forces us to think sociologically about the contextual factors that move these genres. As Lena explains,

I wouldn't say that the individual people don't matter. I would say that a different set of phenomena is revealed when we look at the community as a whole. So, in sociology we talk about this as the sociological imagination. When people become unemployed, for example, we're concerned with the deeply personal impact that has on them and the sometimes unique reasons why they were fired or became unemployed.

But at the same time we're also interested in the societal level, the social problems. And we can find that although the impact of joblessness is very serious on an individual, there are also group impacts when a whole community of people is underemployed or unemployed. Similarly, there are shared causes.

The same thing is true with music; that the deeply personal resonance of music is not something that I want to distract from or detract from. But as a sociologist I'm interested in, How do we make music communities work? How do they change over time? And—almost like a garden—what kind of resources do they need to grow? What's the sunlight? What's the soil mixture that's ideal? So, while there are very specific reasons that things happen to specific communities, the patterns are really strong and really remarkable.

Sociologists are also concerned with how we develop a taste for a particular form of culture, whether it's music, food, fashion, or art. Lena extends this argument to the force of those we surround ourselves with—our communities. Perhaps we have a taste for a certain kind of tribe rather than a certain musical style:

Sociologists know that Americans, and actually people across the globe, have a preference for an increasingly huge variety of different things. We used to find in the middle of the century that when college-educated Americans were pre-sented with a list of musical styles and asked what they like, they would check off one or two: classical and opera. But if you do the same thing today with college graduates, they click off everything: bluegrass, rap music. As sociologists, we've just realized that this phenomenon is going on and we're trying to figure out some of the reasons for it. A reason-able explanation is the change in our society, the loosening of bonds, the diversification of people who are in the elite. But we need a different set of cultural theories about how people make choices within those categories. Because the truth is that a working-class person in Tennessee who listens to country music buys different albums from the college-educated graduate who listens to country music. They're making distinctions, and it's not just at the level of whether they like country music or not.

By redefining musical genres as community-based, social experiences, Lena points out how our love for a certain nos-talgic song or a specific style of music might be embedded in something much richer than a great melody or three-note noise. Songs, like smells, evoke a particular sense of memory. And these memories are often shaped by the energy of the people who listened with and around you. Music is social experience, even when all those Beats by Dre headphones seem to nestle listeners into their own little worlds.

## PARTICIPANT PROFILE

**Jennifer C. Lena** is in the departments of sociology and arts administration at Columbia University. She is the author of *Banding Together: How Communities Create Genres in Popular Music* (Princeton University Press, 2012) and What Is the What?, a long-standing blog of culture and hilarity.

# TSP tie-in

## culture and the construction of sex, violence, and poverty

I n this section, scholars demonstrated the reciprocal relationship between culture and social life and explored how culture shapes our experience in the social world. They dug beneath surface-level discussions to reveal the underlying, often unspoken realities of our thoughts and interactions.

This attention to culture can provide valuable insight into many other areas of social life, even when it comes to phenomena like sex, violence, and poverty. As an example, visit TheSocietyPages.org to read two posts about the societal repercussions of a culture that glamorizes sex and violence: "Mass Violence and the Media" by Jacqui Frost and Stephen Suh and "Mass Shootings and the 'Man'ifesto" by Evan Stewart. Each elaborates on the links between the seemingly unending acts of gun violence in the United States and idealized forms of masculinity that rest on notions of male entitlement and (sexual) conquest. Material objects such as guns, music, and video games are often pinpointed as the causes of male violence, while the psychological and societal ramifications of a culture that promotes repressive ideals of masculinity *and* femininity are overlooked.

A more cultural approach can also expand our understandings of poverty. For instance, in a roundtable written by Stephen Suh and Kia Hiese, sociologists Mario Luis Small, Kaaryn Gustafson, and Mark Gould look at the relevance of the decades-old "culture of poverty" rhetoric. A much-debated theory that gained notoriety in 1965 with the publication of a policy report by Daniel Patrick Moynihan, the culture of poverty explains a cycle of poverty through the cultural attitudes and behaviors of certain groups (namely, inner-city African Americans). Adopting a critical approach, the roundtable participants choose not to take on the task of proving or disproving Moynihan's ideas. Rather, they discuss the manner in which contemporary debates regarding poverty—most of which are fraught with racist, classist, and sexist overtones—say more about our society and culture as a whole than any one demographic group within them.

Ultimately, these examples showcase the importance of understanding our lived realities by going beyond the taken-for-granted and naturalized, looking instead at the social forces and cultural ideologies constantly and quietly structuring our lives and experiences.

—STEPHEN SUH AND KYLE GREEN

# all together, now: producing fashion at the global level

**CLAUDIO E. BENZECRY**

t's 5:45 A.M. in Hong Kong, or so it says on the flight display. We left New York some seven hours ago and most lights are out in the business cabin, but Nicole Santana is working. She is flying business thanks to an upgrade afforded by the thousands of miles accrued flying from New York to China to oversee design and production for OmShoes, a shoe company. On her screen, she is detailing an early prototype shoe that hasn't come out as she expected. Production needs to widen the strap on the back.

Santana was in the Guangdong Province city to which we are traveling just 10 days ago, but she's returning to make sure production is completed before the Chinese lunar New Year. The season (in fashion time) for these shoes is actually nine months from now, but schedule is everything. Production is organized around six collections plus up to three clusters of additional products added in by sales request throughout the year. After a 16-hour flight, Santana will hit the ground running. A local driver will take her straight to Om's design office to flesh out details with the design managers in one of the factories her company does business with. She will arrive there around 3:30 A.M. eastern time.

Once Santana feels the design is finalized, she will return to New York City. She expects to stay in Guangdong Province for five days. After four years of working in the company, she has realized that it is better to break what used to be long trips (between two and three weeks) into smaller units. The first trip is 10 days, then, a couple of weeks later, she makes a second trip to correct the prototypes she and her team worked on during the first trip. This lets her ensure the samples are made to satisfaction before they're sent to the United States to be shown to buyers and eventually produced and distributed. Santana is in constant contact with two of the factories in China, one factory with its main design office in Miami, and the owners and president of the company, who live on the U.S. West Coast. This means that, as she wakes up on our first full day in China, Santana can take advantage of the time differences to check on a project she left in the hands of two associate designers back in New York. It's 6:00 P.M. there, and her team will have not yet left the office. When she is in New York, Santana regularly comes home from work after 7:00 P.M., ready for one last round of e-mails with detailing and corrections around 10:00, once the China office has opened.

In this short description of one senior designer's schedule, I've managed to mention several cities, three time zones, and nine seasons. This is how—and when—fashion production happens.

## how do we study cultural production at the global level?

The literature on globalization and culture is currently divided among three primary approaches: macro level, meso level, and micro level. The macro-level perspective, often referred to as the *cultural/media imperialism thesis,* pays close attention to the influence of powerful actors, institutions, and states on powerless actors, institutions, and states (e.g., citizens of economically disadvantaged countries). Such approaches find inequalities in cultural exchange, patterns of ownership, and access to infrastructure and technological resources, often concluding that globalization destroys cultural diversity and undermines the vitality of indigenous culture.

A related perspective operates at the meso level. These studies attend to how city and state bureaucracies organize cultural and economic policy. Authors adopting this perspective emphasize the political economy of globalization in which policy and trade decisions shape local cultural experiences and provide a window into the organizational context in which cultural objects are produced and circulated. Similar to macro perspectives, this literature establishes a top-down research strategy that reveals little about the actors who mediate multiple levels of production and reception.

Empirically oriented micro-phenomenological approaches have recently challenged the cultural imperialism and top-

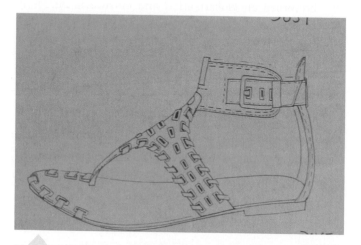

A drawing photographed in the course of my study.
© Claudio Benzecry

down paradigms. The advantage of this approach is its ability to observe the local dissemination and consumption of cultural goods. This research aims to show the connections between the macro and the micro with a strategy anthropologist George Marcus has called "follow the thing." It focuses on the various levels of production, circulation, and use of fashion objects in multiple scenarios. Here, I take this third approach, using actual cultural objects—shoes—to demonstrate the round-the-clock schedule of global design and production.

It is worth noting that cultural sociologists like myself tend to study designers instead of sweatshop workers, whom labor-oriented sociologists (and activists) have rightly emphasized. This alternative focus has three main contributions to make to our understanding of the global production of culture. The first one is that the globalization and commodity chain literature has hidden how intertwined design and production are. Too often this means that all we get to see is that raw materials and supply become a finalized product, in an almost automatic fashion, without an account of all the work it takes to go from one to the other. Second, by looking at designers we get to see how all the networks are pulled together to create one finalized product in a way that would be impossible to observe from the end point of a factory worker. Third, the vantage point of the designer allows us to highlight the temporal incongruity of assembling products on a global scale.

## where does design happen?

The production of manufactured goods happens through coordination among many different locales. Scholars who follow every step along the way, studying where the far-flung components come from and how they are assembled until they are finalized, circulated, and consumed, call this a *commodity chain*. The existence of a global factory is not a given but rather the work of many people and institutions that connect different parts of the production and circulation processes. The global supply and production chains are contingent on many people and require flexibility, cooperation, and speed. Executive fiat or managerial omniscience have little to do with getting a fashion designer's sketch to the runway.

In fact, it's sometimes hard to pinpoint where and when design happens. Does it start when designers assemble drawings and inspiration boards in their offices, hoping to make sense of how they work as a collection? Maybe it's earlier, when designers are traveling to Europe and a few major shopping districts in the United States (mostly in Los Angeles, New York, and Miami) to look for inspiration in shoes, belts, buckles, and accessories. Or even before that, when—

scouting very expensive online trend forecasting services—companies like Om pay for the latest pictures of Milan's runway shows, the window displays of Paris's trendy Le Marais neighborhood, or a heavily stylized woman's street fashion in Yokohama, Japan?

When designers synthesize all that global information, they create mood boards, putting together a story line about the colors and materials they will use to imagine their potential customers. Are they neoromantics? Tomboy chic? The drawing process will help those moods and each shoe

A trend forecasting service supplies photos of fashion-forward looks on the street. © Claudio Benzecry

Parisian style photo taken on a fashion trip.
© Claudio Benzecry

model intersect. Designers must also take into account which shoes will replace those from previous collections. Is there a sandal for the West Coast buyers? What about a crazy or conceptual shoe that a couture lover could take from the runway to a gala? Throughout this process, regardless of whether the conversation is sited within a shopping trip to Berlin, an image from a São Paulo street, or a physical meeting in the Pacific Northwest, the same people discuss information and trend reports; imagine how the many buckles, shoes, watches, and swatches they bought can become shoes;

correct drawings; and discard up to 70 percent of the designers' initial work (for a final collection of 35 shoes, designers draw up more than 100).

## where does production happen?

Production is constant. It happens simultaneously in many places. The beginning of the chain I followed starts at company headquarters on the West Coast and in New York, where most of the design team works (in fact, where most design teams work—including those of French Connection, Kenneth Cole, Coach, BCBG Max Azria, Sam Edelman, Frye, and Steve Madden). It's no mistake that designers cluster together: They need to socialize and brainstorm with other designers, there must be good schools that provide companies with an influx of young talent (in New York, Parsons The New School of Design is queen, but SUNY's Fashion Institute of Technology and even the Pratt Institute send talented graduates into companies like OmShoes), and there have to be shared services and expert knowledge that can circulate among the firms that make up the fashion ecology.

The first production decision the CEO and the head designers make is how many collections there will be in a year (lately, from four to nine, though the timing between collections is blurred by a now-constant design process demanded by the fast fashion market). Then they decide on the number of lines per collection and which consumers they are designing for. When making these decisions, the firm is also choosing which companies will provide the shoes' components (e.g., leather, insoles, and accessories) and which sample rooms and factories will build the prototypes (the first versions of the shoe, usually done with discarded materials and scraps), the sale samples (the ones Om uses to gauge interest from potential buyers in seasonal fashion shows), and the confirmed samples for quality and design. In 2013, Om made 2.5 million pairs of shoes, all of which emerged from these many minute decisions.

The factories (in this case, in China, India, and Mexico) also compete to participate in this production process. They do so via agents, who coordinate the match between shoe company and factory by offering to produce samples, thus showing off the quality of the shoes they make. The factories are specialized and produce only shoes. Om's factories are located in three places: Leon, Mexico, where the men's collection is produced, to take advantage of the local craft industry's talent with leather products and the favorable exchange rate; in Chennai, India, where the cheapest line, made of leather and less noble materials like plastic, is developed; and in Guangdong Province, where most of the volume of production (for both Om and OMA!, the company's diffusion line and high-end line, respectively) takes place. As much as this all happens globally, there is local competition. In

China, northern provinces such as Shaanxi compete against the special economic zones in Guangdong and Fujian. Even within Guangdong Province, cities like Shenzhen, Dongguan, and Guangzhou compete to become the province's center of shoe production.

Now, what does production look like to the designer? While I've been able to map all the macro components of how a shoe is produced, the day-to-day work of putting the shoe together is a little bit messier. Let's follow one shoe to see how it works.

A drawing with instructions and a second file, including a sample request in an Excel spreadsheet with precise descriptions of the pattern, binding, laces, studs, eyelets, zipper puller, button buckles, zippers, and upper stitching as well as the lining, insole binding, sock, sock stamp, heel, welt, outsole, and so on, are sent to one of Om's factories in Dongguan.

Once that first shoe gets developed into a prototype, Nicole Santana receives an e-mail with a picture and detailed information, along with a picture of the shoe on the foot model in the sample room. After close scrutiny, Santana draws corrections onto the images. Now the main factory in China must triangulate that information with a development company in Miami that partially owns the factory. Corrections may last several rounds of design and material issue changes, but shoes do not go into production until the sample is confirmed.

they owned factories in Taiwan in the 1970s (when "Made in Taiwan" was in every garment you could get your hands on) and, later, the South Korean factories fueling the early round of globalized sneaker production. As production costs lowered in China, the Taiwanese entrepreneurs invested in Dongguan. Thus it's not unusual while in Guangdong Province to meet with agents, quality-control officers, and technicians who are all of Taiwanese origin. Sample room managers, on the other hand, are Chinese: They need to be able to communicate with the local workers.

In many popular accounts of globalization, the world appears frictionless or flat. The idea is that production is always ready to be moved into any country or area that makes itself cheaply available. But previous infrastructure and knowledge matter. As I've observed Taiwanese factory owners (and their cadres of experts) producing shoes for decades and making careful choices about where to do so, so, too, are global pharmaceutical companies developing high-cost drugs particular about where they conduct medical experiments. These medical trials tend to happen in Eastern European countries like Poland or in technocratic Brazil, where there is a system of physicians in place who can centralize the supply of patients needing the medicine and find appropriate medical facilities and certified doctors.

This changeability of geography is both a hallmark of globalized production and a symbol of how flexible and responsive supply chains have become. For instance, a look at the production of other low-technology and labor-intensive industries, like garment or furniture production, shows what sociologists have called a *virtuous cycle* of production. Spanish apparel company Zara, given the nature of fast fashion, does not bring in products from Southeast Asia like its competitors; what they save in transportation costs, they can spend in salary and technology. As competing countries like Portugal, Morocco, and Turkey improve their technology, Zara changes the locations of its main suppliers.

© Claudio Benzecry

A similar process can be observed in countries that started out producing low-tech, labor-intensive products like T-shirts. As local salaries grew, entrepreneurs divested their money by either shifting into more refined clothing or, as working conditions improved and unions formed, into low-end electronics assembly. Something like this is happening in Dongguan. Lately, it's become too expensive for international production; some capitalists are starting to invest in electronics instead of shoes. Those who stick with shoes are moving into China's northern provinces, where salaries and production costs are lower.

## where do supplies come from?

Of course a shoe needs to be made out of something—or some things. There is great variation in terms of where in the world parts come from. Om hires an Italian agent from Milan to coordinate the global materials and make sure they get to the design companies. Most of the higher-quality shoes are built with leather from the two tanneries the Italian company owns in Tuscany. Other higher-price-point shoes are made from leather sourced in south Brazil (from Franca, in the state of São Paulo, and Novo Hamburgo, in the state of Rio Grande do Sul). For Om's other shoes, leathers are sourced from Chengdu, in Sichuan Province, or from India (Chennai) and Thailand (though the carcasses processed in Thailand's

Samut Prakan Province actually come from Buenos Aires, Argentina). So it is that one Italian leather supply agency descrambles a global network of suppliers and producers, sometimes by linking Om directly with suppliers that fully finalize the leather on their own, sometimes by supplying carcasses to tanneries, sometimes by working and reworking lower-quality leathers in their own tanneries, and sometimes by simply supplying their own Italian product.

## when do design and production happen?

Put simply, design happens all the time. It's a 24-hour cycle that includes both e-mail and live presence. If a shoe is first drawn in New York, there is a constant exchange of e-mails with headquarters in the West (in the Pacific time zone) and with Om's China office. Santana's team works to consider pricing and consumer constraints that will take a shoe off their list. For the shoes that move forward, the team must gather an immediate analysis of whether the factories in China can produce such shoes and whether the materials are available. This means that, if a day started when Santana woke up in New York, went to the office, and checked the e-mails that came in from Dongguan, that day *never actually ended*. Santana's first morning e-mail answers queries and concerns about scheduling and capabilities in China. Later, as she arrives at her office, her team works to make sense of the constraints and developments signaled by the China office. Past noon, they contact the West Coast with updates on the designs. Essentially, communication subsumes Santana's entire day. Before going to bed, she will spend another hour furiously e-mailing as South China wakes up and begins its workday.

This 24/7 dynamic has affected many industries. Take, for example, architecture, with firms in Europe and the United States shifting work schedules when developing projects in

Sample room in Dongguan. © Claudio Benzecry

Southeast Asia to make themselves available to the clients and local builders in real time. So if one week an architectural team is working on a U.S. project and operates from 10:00 A.M. to 7:00 P.M., its timing shifts to develop a residential complex in Istanbul (with those workers committed to the project arriving earlier than the rest of the team), and it absolutely changes if the client is a mall in Hong Kong. For that, teams will arrive at the office at 7:00 P.M., ready for an all-nighter. Nevertheless, no industry has been more affected by the restructuring of time than financial services, with firms in London virtually making time into money, because their time zone gives a competitive advantage, allowing them to be open—albeit briefly—at the same time as both the Tokyo and the New York City stock exchanges, services, and banks.

The cycle of production in the fashion industry has actually intensified lately. The influx of fast fashion companies (like Zara, Forever 21, H&M, and Topshop) has destroyed the old-fashioned cycle of four seasons with intermittent mini-collections. Now if a piece has gone down a high-fashion runway anywhere in the world, the inexpensive (or less-expensive) version of it is expected in stores within weeks. Om now has nine annual collections. A second development that affects the temporality of production is that most work is now done in terms of projects rather than workdays. There's little concern for an established workweek or work hours, predictable vacation days, and the combination of work and leisure people expect in a highly skilled occupation like clothing design. This is true in similar industries like architecture, media, and advertising. The most tragic exemplar is the recent death of a copywriter in a Singapore ad agency: He died after working for three days straight. There just wasn't time for sleep.

A shoe is a great conduit for seeing the global dynamics at play in the production of an economic good. And while these dynamics are easier to understand with products that need intensive technology and transform raw materials into a final product, globalization is also affecting natural, unprocessed items like fruits and vegetables, as well as immaterial products, like pharmaceutical or medical expertise. To close, I want to call attention to something Americans consume as readily as shoes: sushi.

High-quality tuna, the kind that is served in expensive restaurants in New York, London, and Paris, is brought in from the main market in Tokyo, Tsukiji, while actually fished in the North Atlantic, either on the shores of New England and Halifax or near the Strait of Gibraltar (the highly migratory tuna is sold to middlemen who send the highest quality fish to Tokyo). Time zone differences play a crucial role in the circulation of this fish because buyers (mostly Japanese) call the Tsukiji market, where the auction has just concluded, and

Leather samples in Om's Dongguan office. © Claudio Benzecry

jumbo jets and high-tech refrigeration ensure fresh fish is sent around the world daily. Fish from south Spain, where it is actually trapped, put into a pen, and fed, also makes it to Tokyo, where its global value will be set by expert buyers (much like the fashion buyers who can distinguish among different qualities of leather, these fish experts can distinguish among qualities of fish). Industrial fishing happens in coordination with the demand of the Tokyo market, so much that it affects local production and consumption elsewhere. Sometimes tuna is fished to replace good stock that is being exported to Japan; some Spanish tuna ends up in U.S. supermarkets, replacing the American tuna that was exported to Japan; and in some cases, U.S. tuna comes back from Japan, certified by quick circulation through the Tsukiji marketplace.

Whether it's fish or fashion, globalization is happening everywhere, all the time.

## RECOMMENDED READING

Theodor C. Bestor. 2001. "Supply-Side Sushi: Commodity, Market, and the Global City." *American Anthropologist* 103(1): 76–95. Describes how Tokyo's Tsukiji market mediates multiple, worldwide locations, culinary fashions, and the fish industry to produce sushi at a global scale.

Sidney Mintz. 1986. *Sweetness and Power: The Place of Sugar in Modern History*. New York: Penguin. Traces the history of sugar production and consumption, showing its links to slavery, class ambition, and industrialization.

Adriana Petryna. 2009. *When Experiments Travel: Clinical Trials and the Global Search for Human Subjects*. Princeton, NJ: Princeton University Press. Brings together the players in clinical trials, from corporate laboratories in the United States to research and public health sites in Poland or Brazil, to show

how commercial medical science is integrated into local health systems.

Xuefi Ren. 2011. *Building Globalization: Transnational Architecture Production in Urban China*. Chicago: University of Chicago Press. Shows the many ways urbanization and globalization are intertwined in China by studying transnational architectural production in aspiring global cities like Beijing and Shanghai.

Pietra Rivoli. 2009. *The Travels of a T-Shirt in the Global Economy: An Economist Examines the Markets, Power, and Politics of World Trade*. 2nd ed. Hoboken, NJ: Wiley. Following a T-shirt she bought for the holidays, the author untangles the history of the globalization of world trade, specifically in the textile industry.

# part 2

# sociological critiques
of culture

# troubling bodies with abigail saguy, natalie boero, and c. j. pascoe

**KYLE GREEN**

dentity is increasingly tied to the body. Advertisements for natural herbal supplements to improve body shape, scientific concoctions to increase libido, and surgical procedures guaranteed, if not required, to impress sexual partners fill e-mail inboxes on a daily basis. The message is only slightly less overt in more public spaces. For instance, images of celebrities, models, and athletes displaying their chiseled, airbrushed six-pack abs and cellulite-free thighs guide customers down the checkout lane at the local big-box grocery store. Large-font proclamations cover these bodies, suggesting your body and life could be the same, if you'd only buy the magazine and try the trendy new workout or diet explained inside.

While increased understanding of and ability to alter the body is cause for celebration for many, critical scholars, including Bryan Turner and Susie Orbach, have been quick to remind us that these advances have not always led to happiness and health. The ability to conquer flesh and bone continues to place more responsibility on individuals to maintain the proper aesthetic appearance. And, with the exponential growth in the number of "experts"—now including but not limited to medical scientists, nutritional experts, the beauty industry, yoga gurus, and spiritual counselors—the difficulty of making sense of the overwhelming and often contradictory amount of information about health and bodies only grows. While it would be rather crude to suggest that in a different time or in a different place there is or has been a natural body, Orbach's claim that we have entered an era of increased body confusion seems particularly apt.

On the one hand, sociologists have insisted that our relationship to our bodies and the pressure on bodies to fit particular aesthetic ideals cannot be isolated from larger social and economic contexts. For instance, scholars Susan Bordo and Nick Crossley have examined how bodies have moved further and further away from being tools sculpted by manual labor to expressions of personal preference, cultural pressure, and the leisure time to devote to creating a pleasing body (whether it's for yourself or for onlookers). The body has become another object to be prepared for consumption.

Perhaps more important for more culturally oriented sociologists are the subjective and ideological dimensions of shifts in bodies that bring blame and shame or pride and plaudits. Often thought of as the most biological and personal aspect of social life, the body is always already shaped and defined—literally—through culture. In this chapter, I consider two recent talks with experts about framing and defining the proper body.

In the first conversation, Abigail Saguy discusses the dominant cultural frames that stigmatize and attach blame to fatness. Saguy helps us see how the experts we turn to and the language we use to normalize and hide judgment damages others who may not possess the "appropriate" or "ideal" body type.

In the second conversation, Natalie Boero and C. J. Pascoe look more closely at the relationship between people's experience of their bodies and medical ideas of health. The authors take us inside the online world of pro-anorexia communities, showing how the chat rooms create safe spaces in which individuals share knowledge, find support, and engage with and resist institutions condemning their bodies and communities.

The studies approach the cultural construction of the body on two very different scales and from two different methodological approaches. However, both turn to bodies to trouble our notions of propriety, health, and bodies as well as how we see others' bodies and self-presentation as illustrative of deeper aspects of the self, including moral fortitude and mental ability.

*Saguy began by discussing the importance and difficulties of language about bodies.*

**Abigail Saguy:** There's a lot of stigma and discrimination against people who are heavy and so, unsurprisingly, there's confusion and disagreement about how to best talk about it. I avoid using the words *obese, obesity, overweight* unless I'm talking about how other people use those terms. The reason I do is because one of the main goals of this book [*What's Wrong with Fat?*] is to problematize the common ways of talking about fatness as a medical problem and a public health crisis . . . all of these terms take for granted what I call a "medical frame" or a "public health crisis frame." If you think about it, try to imagine someone who is obese and healthy. It's inconceivable; it doesn't make sense because the word *obesity* already implies medical pathology. And so it makes certain things unthinkable, and these are precisely the things that I'm trying to get people to think about. Why do we medicalize and pathologize fatness? Is there another way of talking about it? Overweight? Over what weight? *Overweight* assumes that there's a normative weight, a good weight and one can be over that weight and being over that weight is, again, a medical problem.

I use the terms *fat* and *fatness*. And this is not a perfect solution either . . . but I'm taking a cue from the fat-acceptance movement that has reclaimed *fat* and *fatness* as neutral descriptors. This is a common tactic of social movements. We saw this with the Black Power movement, reclaiming *black* as a neutral or even positive term; with *queer*; and we also see it with *fat*. I sometimes talk about "heavy" and "heavier." Sometimes I use the word *corpulence*. Other words that people use I don't use because they have argued, and I agree, that they're euphemistic, which also implies that there's something wrong with fat.

*Saguy continued by reflecting on how discrimination against fatness is often overlooked.*

**Saguy:** We are in the midst of a burgeoning discourse on obesity and the obesity epidemic, and that this is a major public health crisis. And that discourse takes for granted, again, the idea that it is a problem, a medical problem [and] a social problem, to be heavy and the solution is making fat people thin as opposed to, for instance, making thin people less prejudiced against fat.

*Key to understanding the way fatness is treated by society is to examine the way it is framed. Saguy outlines the consequences of some various frames.*

**Saguy:** [P]eople don't even think they are using a frame when they say *obese, obesity, overweight.* They assume they are talking about a fact. . . . And what I try to do in the book [*What's Wrong with Fat?*] is denaturalize that and say let's take a step back and think about how and why we talk about fatness.

. . . So you can think about fatness as a medical problem, and that's going to have implications: People need treatment; they need to change their bodies; maybe they need to take drugs or have surgery. You can think about that; that's the medical frame. Or you can think that [fatness is] a public health crisis. That's become very dominant since—but only since—about 2000. [In this frame], we need to have collective action, government action, to change population weight, to change behavior. . . .

But fatness could also be portrayed as a civil rights issue, in which the problem is not that people, individuals, or the society as a whole are too fat and therefore unhealthy. The problem is that there's bigotry and discrimination on the basis of body size, and the solution is not to make fat people thinner but to make the society at large more tolerant and even celebrate body size diversity.

[H]ow we frame this issue has very different implications for policy as well as for individual interactions and behaviors and for people's lives. We're all affected by this issue in different ways. Those who are heavy, especially women, are most penalized by this; [they] face discriminations, they are taunted, their dignity is denied on an everyday basis with strangers and intimate relationships with doctors. Those who are thinner, again especially women—though this affects men, especially gay men— live in fear of becoming fat. And this can also be a real tyranny in their lives. These symbolic distinctions have huge material consequences.

*What about the connections people make between fatness and moral failings?*

**Saguy:** Peter Stearns, in his book *Fat History*, shows that at the end of the nineteenth century it was considered beautiful and desirable, especially for women, to be heavy. It's about the turn of the century that it becomes cast as immoral. . . . This history is somewhat contested. There's a new book coming out, but it's very clear at least that we start seeing a strong moral argument about fatness at the beginning of the twentieth century. [It's seen] as a sign of sloth and gluttony. This has not gone away. Now it's combined with the medical and public health crisis frame. So, people talk about people who are eating themselves to death: they are eating too much, they are gluttonous, they are slothful, *and* it has medical implications.

*The moral judgment of fatness is often raced, classed, and gendered. It bears more than a passing similarity with the language used to decry welfare.*

**Saguy:** Weight is highly correlated with economic status; this is especially true for women. Once we consider, among people who take for granted that being fat is a medical problem, a public health crisis, who is blamed? Who is held responsible? I call these *blame frames.* The most dominant one in the U.S. context is that of personal responsibility. Here it's the individual fat people who just can't push away from the table.... [T]he discourse is very similar in terms of the "welfare queens" and just poor people in general and their insatiable appetites. It's very raced as well as classed, and politically it is used to say, "Well, should we be giving these people food stamps?"... It becomes a way of blaming the poor for their misfortune, for their health problems, as opposed to discussing the way, for instance, economic inequality or poverty leads to poor health outcomes.

*The use of blame frames by media and public health outlets, Saguy tells TSP, only exacerbates the problem.*

**Saguy:** All this discussion on the obesity epidemic may be worsening stigma. And this is not just a social justice concern, but it's also a health concern because we know that being the object of discrimination and stigma has negative effects on cortisol levels, on blood pressure, and ultimately on heart disease and life expectancy.

Many people, especially heavy women, perceive the doctor's office as a hostile environment. They're not treated with dignity. They are told that whatever health problems they are presenting have to be due to their weight (and . . . that it's their fault). . . . This can be a life or death situation if a test could have discovered a [treatable] problem and instead the doctor says, "Come back when you've lost 50 pounds."

. . . The fact that [New Jersey's] Chris Christie could not be a serious candidate [for the U.S. presidency] unless he lost weight is very telling. . . . "If he can't control his weight, how can he run the country?" It's definitely a moral judgment.

The way that he justifies health [as the] reason [for having Lap-Band surgery] is very common. The socially accepted account of why people are losing weight [is that] they are losing weight to be healthy. But actually, a colleague of mine, Paul Campos . . . asked people if they could live longer, would they gain weight to add five years of their lives? They would not. But they were willing to give up years of life to lose weight. Again, it was not a random sample . . . but it suggests that losing weight for health reasons is what people think is *acceptable*, but it's not the real motivation. . . . It's interesting now that we have our first black president, to ask, "Could we have a fat president?" Is the prejudice so great, still so great, that it would not be possible?

*Where there are powerful frames, there are often opportunities for resistance to those frames. Saguy explains some efforts to offer alternative, more positive framing options for fatness.*

**Saguy:** We have a strong tradition in the U.S. of talking about group-based discrimination, [but] there's very little discussion of weight-based discrimination, and I think this is largely because the frames of medical problem and public health crisis are so dominant. The assumption . . .

is that we have to make fat people thin [rather than accept them at their size]. The other two frames I talk about are the beauty frame in which, this comes from the idea of "Rubenesque," . . . fat is beautiful; . . . some are trying to reclaim that . . . [and] the "health at every size" frame. This is something that is very increasingly important among clinicians. And we see it among those who work with eating disorders as well as nutritionists and doctors. The idea that it's not unhealthy to be fat, that you can be healthy at any size. We don't want to treat the fatness; we want to, for instance, get people more active and tell them they can be active at any size. When we try to get people to exercise or change their diet to lose weight it's usually unsuccessful. . . . We'd do better to just focus on improving health.

*While Boero and Pascoe also have an interest in the way weight, fat, and the body are framed, they take a different approach by examining web-based pro-anorexia communities.*

**Natalie Boero and C. J. Pascoe:** Pro-anorexia communities are, in general, an online phenomenon. They have migrated from e-mail lists to individual websites and discussion groups, and they've cycled through various social networks, of different social networks, just like everything else has. They're some sort of group, an interactive group, where members coalesce around an identity as being pro-anorexic. They identify as being eating disordered, having an eating disorder, but they generally see it as more of a lifestyle. They are generally not involved in any sort of treatment; many of them have never undergone any sort of treatment. They are looking for mutual support in crafting a pro-anorexia lifestyle and building a community.

Because of the ephemeral qualities of the site and the migration of members from site to site so quickly, it's next to impossible to get any sort of accurate count on how many people participate. But if you plug "pro-anorexia" or "pro-ana" into any sort of Google search, you will find hundreds if not thousands of sites.

*Perhaps, not surprisingly, the sites have been a source of negative response and controversy.*

**Boero and Pascoe:** It comes from politicians, parents, sufferers of eating disorders. For instance, in France there have been a lot of discussions about getting laws passed that make it illegal to encourage extreme weight loss in online communities. In the United States we haven't seen laws passed per se, but Tumblr just came out with a statement with their goal of taking down these sorts of pro-eating disorder websites, or microblogs, on their site. You see online service providers also trying to sort of get rid of these sites, even if they're not technically against the law. This is not new. Yahoo! was pressured to take down these sites 10 or 12 years ago. And interestingly, it's also feminists who have very much had a negative response to these sites.

*And, while the sites are not without fault, according to Boero and Pascoe, much of the criticism focuses on the most extreme aspects of the pro-anorexia communities.*

**Boero and Pascoe:** I think overwhelmingly the media has whipped up sort of a moral panic around these [websites]. I don't mean to sound glib here; eating disorders are a serious issue. [But the media has] sort of taken the most sensational aspects of these sites and put them out there as the ground zero for how people develop eating disorders these days. There's been a very sensational reaction that has focused largely on the supposed desire of veteran members wanting to recruit. . . . As these being breeding grounds for anorexia and bulimia and other disorders . . . as very predatory. [It's] a very decontextualized moral panic, which is probably the definition of a moral panic. But really, [pro-ana sites have] largely been taken out of context, and the more sensational aspects have been focused on.

*In contrast to these popular accounts, Boero and Pascoe seek a deeper understanding of the sites in their research.*

**Boero and Pascoe:** The year and a half [we spent] looking at these sites really gave us a chance to look at the nuances. . . .

We are absolutely guilty of looking at these sites and thinking, "Oh my goodness, this is horrific! This is awful!" It did take us time—a lot of time, in fact—and I think if we had rushed and tried to get an article out as fast as possible, we would have been guilty of some of the things the mainstream media is doing in terms of not seeing things in context. I think that one of the things that [makes our research sound is how we became] so familiar with the conversations, the images, and the ideas posted on these sites over time, getting past the initial shock value . . . to see how a lot of the discussion mirrors more mainstream ideas about weight and weight loss and obesity. And that, to a certain extent, to understand the moral panic around pro-anorexia groups outside of the moral panic of obesity would be a missed opportunity because, if you look on these sites, once you get past some of the more extreme examples, what they're telling each other to do is exactly what [mainstream society is] telling fat people to do. [Take] what we see as problematic in these communities, cut and paste it into a Weight Watchers website and it's seen as legitimate practice around legitimate weight loss.

*Boero and Pascoe explain that it is important for members of pro-anorexia communities to establish authenticity, but it's complicated by the disembodied nature of a site about bodies.*

**Boero and Pascoe:** Rituals are important, but some of the more concrete ways people [assert their legitimacy in these forums] is by displaying their knowledge about the disorders. Talking about their weight and statistics, talking about various side effects that they are experiencing from these disorders that would be characteristic of "real" anorexia. It's a lot of constant reiteration of talking about their bodies, sharing images of their bodies, and using diagnostic categories to frame their bodies online and challenging other people's characterizations of their bodies as well.

Some of the groups we observed required that their participants post or have pictures of themselves as their avatar picture or on their site to ensure authenticity. But a lower percentage actually posted pictures of themselves on the discussion groups because a minority of group members actually posted on the discussion groups themselves [the others tend to read the sites and message boards without contributing]. That's true across the board; there are more people who are members of discussion groups than actually post on them. [Still], if someone challenged your claim to bodily authenticity, you needed to produce a picture. And that didn't even necessarily mean you needed to be successful. Someone could post a picture of themselves at a weight that they weren't happy with, as long as they then did the interactional work of saying, "I'm fat and I want to be skinny." It was more about participating in the discourse than proving you were actually skinny. You had to say you wanted to be skinny . . . or prove you are skinny.

[Surprisingly, these sites revealed] incredibly high levels of aggression. They were constantly policing the boundaries, and that's where the "wanna-orexic" comes in. But they were also very intent on giving each other support in a kind way, in a sometimes humorous way, and sometimes in a mildly aggressive way. If one participated in the discourse correctly, one could elicit all sorts of support. If one didn't participant in the discourse correctly, that's when you could get called out for being "wanna-orexic," or not really anorexic.

*Once a member has established authenticity, Boero and Pascoe explain, the pro-anorexia communities offer a nonjudgmental space and a wide range of resources for people who want to change their bodies. They report website members sharing dieting tips and ways to hide your eating disorder, how to handle your relationships, and what to do when another member doubted their commitment to body modification or sought help for their disordered eating.*

**Boero and Pascoe:** A lot of times this support wasn't just support in developing and maintaining anorexia. But a lot of it had to do with managing symptoms, what to eat, what not to eat, dealing with family members and friends who were concerned about your eating habits.

We would usually see support for whatever people wanted support for. If someone was going into an inpatient program, people would say, "Good luck, I hope you get better." But if people's parents were forcing them to go into an in-patient program, they would say, "We're so sorry you're going through this. Parents don't understand; nobody understands this." If a person had established themselves as authentically eating disordered, not just looking for a diet, they generally received support for whatever they asked for support for.

*Participants also used the space to share medical knowledge and critique the popular framing of anorexia as a disorder.*

**Boero and Pascoe:** Any one of [the active members of the pro-ana forums] could calculate a BMI for you and any one of them could tell exactly what vitamins and minerals you need to survive and how you could avoid certain side effects. I think the Internet has brought the democratization of medical information in a broad sense, and I think that these participants have certainly been taking advantage of that. And they know in a way what they're dealing with. Obviously this is not to say that people can "manage" their eating disorders or that there are no harmful effects—sometimes the medical advice seems to be wrong or the poster is challenged on it, but they certainly employ a lot of medical language.

We actually see that the participants on these sites have a variety of dispositions about their disorders. Some participants are very open saying that this is a disorder and they want to recover from it; others are very assertive in saying they see this as a lifestyle choice, that there's nothing to recover from, that it's not a disease. We see the same participant, the same person, posting along both of these lines, really teasing out the ambivalence. . . .

That is again one of those findings that took time, that sort of came to us later in the process. We were sort of frustrated that it's not all "pro-ana, pro-ana, pro-ana"! It's actually some fairly complex feelings and thoughts and analysis being shared out there about eating disorders. If some of the goals of our research is to really think about how we can address eating disorders as a social problem, then understanding that we aren't dealing with a very cut-and-dried [issue] . . . is very important.

*Boero and Pascoe closed by underscoring that there is no one-size-fits-all model of anorexia, nor is there a one-size-fits-all model for preventing and healing disordered eating. Anorexia as a disease does not, in other words, need to be dropped as a medical or media frame, but the public, the media, the medical community, and individuals need a greater appreciation of nuance and competing expectations about acceptable, desirable body types.*

**Boero and Pascoe:** I think it is important to think about the population we are studying. We are studying a largely nonclinical population, which is, in part, what makes this study unique. Among eating disorders, most research has been done among clinical populations. I think what it simply means is that you can't use earlier characterizations of anorexics based on in-patient studies to characterize pro-ana anorexics. You can't simply graft on one to the other. It's a lot more complex.

We have a certain understanding of the person who becomes anorexic, but the communities we've been studying who engage in these practices (mostly women) were a lot more varied than these characterizations—primarily of clinical populations—would indicate.

Obviously, we are a society that has a fraught relationship around bodies and food. . . . We [also] live in a society that tends to individualize. We tend to look for eating disorders in individuals or very small groups or we focus in and blame one structure, like the media. Both have been part and parcel of how we've thought about anorexia, bulimia, and other eating disorders, and both approaches really miss the larger social context.

## PARTICIPANT PROFILES

**Natalie Boero** is in the sociology department of San Jose State University. She is the author of *Killer Fat: Media, Medicine, and Morals in the American Obesity Epidemic* (Rutgers University Press, 2012).

**C. J. Pascoe** is a sociologist at the University of Oregon. She is the author, with Natalie Boero, of *Anas, Mias, and Wannas: Identity and Community in a Pro-Ana Subculture* (University of Michigan Press, 2014).

**Abigail Saguy** is in the departments of sociology and gender studies at the University of California, Los Angeles. She is the author of *What's Wrong with Fat?* (Oxford University Press, 2013).

# the homogenization of asian beauty

**C.N. LE**

The old cliché says that beauty is in the eye of the beholder. But who is the beholder? That's complicated when we look through the unique lens of different countries and societies. In a more globalized world, culture, race, media, and power intersect to create an idea of beauty admired by a collective, rather than by an individual.

In my daily browsing of Reddit—the popular online news, humor, and information aggregation site—I did a double take when I saw a submission titled "Korea's Plastic Surgery Mayhem Is Finally Converging on the Same Face: Miss Korea 2013 Contestants." The picture shows 21 pageant contestants later found to be competing in a regional, not national, contest in the city of Daegu. Still, the women's hairstyles and dress differ, but that's about all. Whether it's the effect of popular plastic surgery or the pageant using a single person to Photoshop the headshots—or, more likely, both—these women look virtually the same.

Promotional photos; composite via gawker.com.

To think through this startling homogeneity, a sociologist has to ask why *beauty* would come to mean just one thing in one culture. What does the Korean convergence mean about the racial, ethnic, and cultural aspects of physical beauty around the world? Answering such big questions means looking at the political and gendered context of women's bodies, the historical ideals of beauty and their differences and similarities across countries and societies, how certain beliefs of physical image intersect with cultural stereotypes about Asian Americans, and finally, how ideals of physical beauty are evolving.

## beauty pageants and the male gaze

Whenever we discuss issues and ideals related to physical beauty and women's bodies, we need to be conscious of the "male gaze." In basic terms, the concept refers to heterosexual men objectifying women and judging their value almost entirely on physical characteristics. The male gaze involves seeing women solely as erotic images, two-dimensional tools for the visual pleasure of heterosexual men rather than as human beings with a comprehensive set of thoughts, emotions, and agency. It is within this context that many women and men criticize the existence of beauty pageants altogether: They are often premised on, and result in, the objectification of women, while also reinforcing gender roles and male supremacy.

Just as important, beauty pageants around the world can also result in the homogenization of women. These visual displays are often framed around a set of predetermined norms or prevailing opinions about what heterosexual men consider attractive or erotic. Often, these predominant attributes are very narrowly focused and defined, leaving little room for variations or exceptions. Today, in many countries including the United States, the general beauty standard for women includes physical characteristics such as a triangular-shaped face, small nose, high cheekbones, long legs, small waist, moderately sized breasts, curvaceous thighs, and a "proper" proportion among the latter three (that is, a less exaggerated form of the hourglass figure lauded in earlier decades). This is not to say that many men and women do not appreciate and covet different physical standards, only that this is the dominant cultural standard. Those with preferences for, say, bodies with three limbs rather than four, narrow hips, or broader measurements in any portion of the body are considered outside the norm—even, to the extreme, fetishists.

Taken together, the male gaze in general and beauty pageants in particular set the stage for modern societies to equate physical appearance and a specific attractiveness with value judgments of superior versus inferior, normal versus abnormal, and good versus bad (or even evil). In our particular discussion of the Miss Korea 2013 contestants, these cultural elements intersect with the historical and political dynamics of race and ethnicity.

## what constitutes physical and cultural beauty?

Beauty ideals are sure to be distinct among different racial and nationality groups. Looking at the portraits of the Miss Daegu, Korea contestants brings up the question of whether

Asians and Asian Americans are implicitly or explicitly conforming to dominant, white, Western standards of physical beauty. Let's start with the meaning of light skin tone and regional beauty standards. As historians and other scholars have pointed out, European colonization of non-white countries in Africa, Asia, and Central/South America elevated European history and culture, including the physical appearance of whites as a racial group. This solidified Europeans' position at the top of the political, economic, cultural, and military hierarchy on a global scale. As their culture spread, frequently by means of physical conquest, racially based standards of beauty came to include light-colored hair and eyes and, perhaps most important, light skin. After the United States rose to the top of the global hierarchy in the twentieth century, these European-based images of beauty eventually melded into a general white-based standard of beauty.

Meanwhile, the cultural dynamics and connotations of light skin operate slightly differently within Asian societies. To a certain degree, white images of beauty have been diffused within Asian countries. However, in many Asian societies, the high status associated with light skin has less to do with emulating whites as a racial group than with representing wealth and privilege. Upper-class people would not need to perform manual labor. Being able to hire others to do work in the hot sun left the wealthy indoors in the shade, cultivating a distinct difference between the fair skin of the upper classes and the sun-baked visages of laborers.

The introduction and spread of capitalism and Western culture in the last several decades has added another layer of cultural meaning to light skin in Asian societies. Now it is associated with whites as a racial group and the corresponding aura of *global* wealth, power, and status. In other words, as U.S. political, economic, and cultural influence became widespread after World War II and intensified with the emergence of globalization starting in the 1980s, U.S. political leaders, celebrities, lifestyles, media products, material goods, and appearances became the standards aspired to among many throughout Asia.

Recent observations by mainstream media outlets, bloggers, and social media sites confirm that the preference for light skin is alive and well in many Asian countries. Skin-lightening creams and lotions are as mainstream as lipstick and mascara. Further, plastic and cosmetic surgery and procedures such as breast augmentations, rhinoplasty (nose jobs), collagen lip implants, and blepharoplasty (an eyelid surgery meant to give Asians a more European "double-eyelid" appearance) are commonplace. For example, data from the International Society of Aesthetic Plastic Surgery show that, in 2011, four of the top eight countries in terms of total cosmetic procedures performed were in Asia: China (#3), Japan (#4), South Korea (#7), and India (#8).

Within the Asian American community, the beauty debate has centered on the cultural implications of changing physical appearance and whether it represents a wholesale conforming to white standards of beauty. People ask, "Where—and what—is Asian beauty?" This question is highlighted in a recent segment from ABC's *Nightline* about an increase in Asian supermodels. They are apparently becoming more prevalent on U.S. and international runways, but the fashion industry may have, rather than reified a diverse beauty, simply reinforced racial stereotypes about Asians, such that all Asians look the same.

Of course, there are many perspectives on whether particular cosmetic procedures represent an adherence to Western standards of beauty or an emergent Asian standard. There is, however, some agreement that white ideals dominate media and fashion industries in industrialized nations and influence how young Asian and Asian American women judge themselves and their physical appearance. Within the United States, Asian Americans are a visible racial minority group, and particularly young people and those who live outside Asian-majority enclaves and cities feel palpable pressure to blend in, to avoid being seen as physically or culturally different. Just look at sitcoms: Asian women are presented as largely homogenous, either sexualized or sub-servient. The more Asian a character appears physically, the more you can expect a stereotypical and demeaning portrayal of asexual nerdiness.

Collectively, these pressures can exert stress and take a negative emotional toll on Asian Americans. They can be disastrous for Asian American women in particular. For example, data from the American Psychological Association and the National Alliance on Mental Illness point out that U.S.-born Asian American women between the ages of 15 and 24 have higher rates of depressive symptoms, suicidal thoughts, and suicide attempts than the national average, including white women. Further, pioneering research from Christine C. Iijima Hall published in 1995 and since confirmed by studies published in academic journals such as *Eating Disorders,* the *International Journal of Eating Disorders,* and the *Journal of Nervous and Mental Disease* describe how young Asian Americans are also particularly vulnerable to eating disorders, much of it influenced by pressures to conform to the model minority and idealized beauty images.

## physical homogeneity and the yellow peril

This question of what constitutes physical beauty among Asians and Asian Americans brings up some further implications. The first, mentioned by several commenters on the Reddit post that got me thinking about just why the Miss Daegu contestants all looked so eerily similar, is that the adherence to *one* physical standard seems to reinforce the unfortunate stereotype that all Asians look the same. Sure, there tends to be a certain degree of visual conformity and homogeneity in beauty pageants in general. But, as many Asian Americans can attest, the stereotype that all Asians look the same feeds into an older, more nefarious idea: that we are the "yellow peril." In this historical yet lingering specter, Asians are faceless, an almost subhuman mass bent on attacking, taking over, and destroying U.S. and/or Western society, economy, and culture.

Take, for instance, the magazine advertisement for soap (that's what Uncle Sam is holding in his left hand) shown on the next page. It comes from the 1800s. The image's main focus is Uncle Sam kicking the Chinese out of the country—sending them back toward the squinty-eyed sun in the horizon. The physically indistinguishable Chinese scurrying into the background represent the yellow peril vanquished by American might, individualism, and superiority. The fact that the yellow peril is being vanquished by *soap* not so subtly reinforces the idea that Asians are a dirty scourge, all alike, all undesirable. The massing of Asians into one homogenous group can seem laughable in a vintage ad, but it has led to many tragic instances of blatant bigotry, discrimination, and even violence.

1886 advertisement via Library of Congress. Public domain.

In 1982, the United States—and the world—saw a graphic enactment of the stereotype that all Asians are the same. Vincent Chin, a naturalized U.S. citizen, was murdered in Detroit, Michigan. The country's economy was in a recession, and its auto industry, based in Detroit, had been particularly hard hit. Many Americans accused Japanese automakers such as Toyota, Honda, and Nissan of using unfair trade practices to gain market share in the United States. As they lost jobs, as factories closed, these white Americans resented Japanese success. The yellow peril seemed poised to take over.

Back to Chin. One night he was out with friends in a Detroit bar, celebrating his upcoming wedding. Two white autoworkers, Ronald Ebens and Michael Nitz, assumed Chin was Japanese, and they began taunting him, accusing him of stealing their friends' jobs. A fight erupted and spilled into the street. Ebens and Nitz chased Chin for blocks before cornering him. They beat Chin to death with a baseball bat. For the murder, Ebens and Nitz received only three years of probation and $3,700 in court fees. Public outrage over the lenient sentences eventually persuaded the federal government to try the two men for violating Chin's civil rights. However, after the case was moved to the predominantly white, working-class city of Cincinnati, Ohio, an all-white jury acquitted both men of all charges. The outrage proved impotent.

In this context, when Ebens and Nitz saw Chin, they saw an embodiment of the yellow peril. Asians were nonhuman, a faceless, collective threat that for one moment could be confronted, could be stopped. So beyond the "weirdness" of the 2013 Miss Korea contestants looking physically similar, historical and cultural contexts frame the pictures as downright dangerous: They reinforce the idea that Asians are identical, a homogenous group with no individual members. That's clearly a harmful idea.

## the ironies of multiculturalism

Ironically, globalization, multiculturalism, and increased racial/ethnic diversity in U.S. society have both propagated generic standards *and* pressured societies to be more open and celebratory of more diverse forms of cultural representation. Two recent pageants in the United States offer hopeful indicators of a move away from white-centric notions of beauty: Lebanese American Rima Fakih as Miss USA 2010 and Indian American Nina Davuluri as Miss America 2014. Notably, both are readily identifiable as women of color and have noticeably darker skin tones than their white pageant counterparts. Their wins were significant symbolic steps for quintessential American brands, visible reminders of the country's "melting pot" ideal.

But it is one thing for an individual Asian American woman to win a prestigious beauty pageant and another for Asian Americans as a group to be treated equally and justly as "real" Americans. Just as newsworthy as Fakih and Davuluri's crownings was the racist backlash on social media, complete with declarations that each woman was a terrorist, not an American, and an insult to (white) American society.

Still, the United States may actually be at the forefront of promoting more diverse images of beauty. As the Census Bureau has long predicted, by 2045 or so, non-Hispanic whites will become a minority (they will still be the largest racial group by far, but they will comprise less than 50 percent of the U.S. population compared to groups of color).

This has already happened in states such as California, Texas, and New Mexico. These demographic changes are slowly leading to cultural changes, as people of color are increasingly integrated within U.S. institutions such as politics, business, education, and media and entertainment. We've already seen the popularity of artists and celebrities of color from Chuck Berry to the Jackson 5, Jay-Z, and Oprah Winfrey. Now we're seeing the Asian and Asian American population slowly accepted as cultural mainstays: Hip-hop group Far East Movement had a 2011 chart-topping hit "Like a G6," Psy and his "Gangnam Style" video were ubiquitous in 2012, and K-pop is a fast-growing genre in the United States, highlighted by Girls' Generation winning YouTube's 2013 Video of the Year award for "I Got a Boy." The advertising industry has made notable strides in including more actors of color in their advertisements and promotional material on television, print, and billboards. No longer are the Asians being chased away in the soap ads; now they're shown driving kids to soccer practice in American-made SUVs.

The spillover effect is that, while there's a huge amount of work left to be done (particularly on television), Americans from all backgrounds are becoming more open to a more diverse set of images of physical beauty. Asian societies, however, seem to be lagging behind the United States in terms of their mainstream representations of physical beauty. Visual homogeneity is the norm. Part of this is due to the general racial homogeneity of Asian countries as compared to the United States. But beyond demographics, prevailing cultural norms within many Asian countries still seem to favor facial and bodily uniformity.

If the United States is, indeed, at the forefront of presenting a more democratic view of physical and cultural beauty, Asian countries must play catch-up. Sure, like most people, I can agree that the young women who competed in the Miss Daegu (and, later, the Miss Korea) pageant are attractive. They're pageant contestants; it's kind of their job. Nonetheless, like most people, I see a lot of different kinds of attractive in the world. Beauty can wear more than one face—when millions of beholders make it known.

## RECOMMENDED READING

Shilpa Davé, LeiLani Nishime, and Tasha Oren, editors. 2005. *East Main Street: Asian American Popular Culture*. New York: New York University Press. These essays describe numerous Asian American cultural practices, including their historical meanings and sometimes contested place within mainstream U.S. society.

Youna Kim, editor. 2014. *The Korean Wave: Korean Media Go Global.* New York: Routledge. This anthology takes an in-depth, critical look at the global explosion of K-pop.

Kent A. Ono and Vincent Pham. 2008. *Asian Americans and the Media.* New York: Polity. A comprehensive survey of how Asian Americans have been portrayed in various U.S. media and emerging forms of Asian American self-expression.

Sheridan Prasso. 2006. *The Asian Mystique: Dragon Ladies, Geisha Girls, and Our Fantasies of the Exotic Orient.* New York: Public-Affairs Publishing. By describing the lives of numerous Asian women, this book explores the context of ever-present and hypersexualized stereotypes.

John Kuo Wei Tchen and Dylan Yeats. 2014. *Yellow Peril! An Archive of Anti-Asian Fear.* Brooklyn, NY: Verso. Details the yellow peril phenomenon from the Enlightenment through the 2012 U.S. elections and beyond.

# comic-conned: gender norms in a carnivalesque atmosphere

**NATALIE WILSON**

S an Diego's Comic-Con feels like a huge five-day carnival. Diverse attendees gleefully snap pictures, brave the crowds, and willingly wait in long (sometimes overnight) lines in this annual atmosphere of fantasy, science fiction, geekdom, and celebrity. The creative costumes and the variety of people in them adds to the buzz, and "the Floor" (where comics, games, and other paraphernalia are on display for purchase) pulses with fans who want to meet their artist idols, get autographs, try new games, and fill their swag bags.

If cosplay (essentially, costuming) is the face of Comic-Con, giving it unique features, "the Floor" is more like its body—a massive, complicated space where attendees digest their cultural addiction of choice, whether it be purchasing a Doctor Who bobble-head or a game of Zombie Dice. Despite the dense, hard-to-navigate space of "the Floor"—it can occasionally feel like wading through the zombie-populated terrain of a *Walking Dead* episode—the space is suffused with a palpable sense of anxious excitement.

San Diego resident and long-time attendee of Comic-Con Melissa Molina describes the atmosphere as full of energy and commotion, noting that what really draws her to the event is "all of the people in the convention center" who "may not all agree on what they like" but who come together in a united devotion to all things Con: comics, science fiction and fantasy films, cult TV shows, video games, fandom culture, and, of course, cosplay.

The heady mix of possibilities at such conventions is described as "a megladon shark attacking Godzilla attacking Mothra attacking Tokyo" by blogger Curtis Silver, who notes that "the biggest of these monsters is, of course, the annual San Diego Comic-Con, where film, television, toys, video games and . . . comics explode into the pop culture consciousness on an annual basis." Indeed, the often-quiet convention center oozes people from every door. For the long weekend of the convention, whether on the trolley or in the nearby Gaslamp Quarter, one would be hard pressed to go more than 10 minutes without seeing a Con-goer wearing a telltale badge.

There are many positive interactions surrounding the cosplay and nerd culture features of the Con. In lines, strangers become friends, offering water, holding places in line, sharing their passion for show X or movie Y. They trade mutual compliments about innovative, creative costumes, and you can see humans of all varieties taking photos of costumed attendees, a practice that is usually filled with appreciation and revelry. As professor Heidi Breuer describes it, the visual presentation gives the Con an atmosphere that allows for positive expressions of geekdom, sexuality, and gender expression.

On her experience as a first-time Con attendee, Breuer writes:

> As a feminist, I was a little nervous about what it would be like at the Con . . . because of the reputation of geek culture as male (or masculinist—with its scantily clad women with impossible curves) but I really found it to be quite friendly and welcoming. . . . The ubiquitous presence of cosplayers is one of the (many) things that gives the Con a carnivalesque atmosphere in which certain norms about sexuality (such as who can be considered attractive, who "should" wear revealing clothes, or what it means when someone is wearing a sexy costume) can be tested and perhaps temporarily transcended. But, among all of the costumes and scantily clad women, there also seemed to be a profound acceptance for

the "non-sexy" woman, or the awkward geek who does not perform the various rituals of femininity as expected, which added to the welcoming, carnivalesque atmosphere.

While I agree that Comic-Con allows for at least a partial transcendence of normative performances and expectations surrounding gendered identity, there *is* still a "masculinist" vibe, as Breuer names it. This sometimes transforms carnivalistic revelry into dehumanizing objectification, predatory gazing, and nonconsensual physical interaction. In other words, sexual harassment and assault. Further, though the crowd is diverse in terms of age, race, body size, and gender (women now make up 40 percent of attendees), the panels are predominantly made up of males (particularly white, heterosexual males), as is the media produced around the Con. The glaring juxtaposition of free expression and a highly diverse atmosphere against a misogynist, prurient streak that allows for a sophomoric, leering aspect to even everyday activities like standing in line or attending a panel makes Comic-Con a useful case study of changing gender practices and norms.

Reading Comic-Con as a cultural event that acts as a barometer of gender consciousness (or lack thereof), I argue that, though women are now far more present as both producers and consumers at the Con, the representation of females in the media featured still overwhelmingly fits in with normative codes of femininity, particularly in relation to the sexualization of women that frames them as "to be looked at." Examining the Con in terms of how media production and consumption are both gendered and gendering, I suggest that the lack of representational parity on panels as well as the male gaze that dominates the atmosphere is part and parcel of a culture that is still decidedly *not* postfeminist.

As Comic-Con was envisioned as a male space for its first 25 to 30 years but has become more of a human space in the last 10 to 15 years, it offers an interesting example of shifting ideas about gender and popular culture. While the term *fanboy* used to rule the roost, it is now common to hear *fangirl* or the nongendered *fandom* when discussing the Con attendees. Some have been critical of the loss of this male space, complaining in one way or another that "women ruined Comic-Con." However, the general atmosphere in the last few years has been welcoming of all attendees, not just males. Echoing this acceptance, panel content now includes various woman-centered lineups, for example, "Women Who Kick Ass," "Women in Marvel Comics," "The Witty Women of Steampunk," "Gender in Comics," and "The Most Dangerous Women of Comic-Con." Given that the media Comic-Con features (for instance, games and comics) are still often seen as male, such panels emphasize that women not only star in but also write, direct, and produce media.

Blogger Dame B discusses the whiplash of gender progress and regressive atmospheres in her piece "The Perfect Feminist Utopia and Comic-Con." When a friend asks if women panels are feminist or sexist, she answers by discussing her imagined PFU (perfect feminist utopia), in which "all panels are half male and half female. . . . The characters, the artists, the writers, the fans, the producers and publishers— all half and half. In PFU, a 'Women in Comics Panel' would be an interesting panel, no more or less fraught than any other panel topic." Further, she adds, "There probably wouldn't be a panel on 'Women in Marvel.' It would be too huge of a topic."

A similar point is made by Holly Derr, who, in her piece for *Bitch*, suggests that until everyone realizes "the female experience *is* the human experience," women will be expected to identify with male characters, panels, and so on. Until this point, Dame B argues, "Women in Comics panels are necessary. They provide a space to discuss the issues associated with being a woman, either as an author, artist, fan, or character. Because we're such a tiny minority in the artists/ writers/characters, it's a really vital space for having that conversation."

It is also important to acknowledge that women are no longer at the Con predominantly as "booth babes" but as cosplayers, fans, gamers, volunteers, and staff. This changing landscape comes with some dismay and discomfort—in this, the Con echoes larger societal shifts in gendered norms and expectations that some welcome (feminists, progressives, social justice advocates) and others disdain (conservatives, the religious right, and yes, many male gamers). Why hasn't the move from hired booth babe to active attendee eradicated the sexist dynamics wherein women are framed as passive, objectified bodies to be ogled?

In some ways, the higher concentration of female attendees has heightened such gazing. The Con may no longer be made up of predominantly male fans desirous to "consume" females via comic books, sexualized characters, or booth babes, yet culture at large still sexualizes girls and women in accordance with the heterosexual male gaze. As such, the often very racy content and costumes of Comic-Con are not aberrant, but they are far more up close and personal. It is one thing to watch Lara Croft on your gaming screen, another to see a near-naked, real-life version of her.

Is it any wonder that the consumers of the media featured at Comic-Cons learn to objectify? Granted, males are also sexualized in such media, but they are often the lead roles. Consumers (especially male ones) are encouraged to envision themselves as strong, muscular, weapon-wielding heroes. Female characters and female consumers are, conversely, more often encouraged to view themselves as desirable, able to trade on sexuality to get ahead in a game or in a fictional world. Sure, there are many action heroines, but they are not nearly as common as the busty comic book vixen or the gaming character whose "armor" leaves her nearly naked.

Harassment is such an enduring concern that various organizations now work with the Con to include antiharassment policies. And the sexualization aspect of the Con is redolent both at the level of the big-business aspects of the event—the film, TV, celebrity, and merchandise promotions—as well as the individual level. While flaunting one's love of geek culture takes various forms, the atmosphere can make an attendee feel more like a jostled piece of meat than a fun-loving fan at a comic carnival.

Misogyny is as common as Stormtrooper costumes at the Con. In lines, one is forced to listen to sexist banter, jokes about "tapping that," and egregious uses of the term *raped* as a supposedly innocuous verb ("Dude, I totally raped that sandwich"). As an example, at the 2013 San Diego Comic-Con I was in line for Hall H (where all the biggest and most buzzed about panels take place) with my 14-year-old daughter. Two very tall white men were behind us, encroaching on our space more and more. Immune to my suggestion that they were practically in our laps, one man proceeded to start bragging about the pee bag he had taped to his leg so he didn't have to leave the line. Then he moved on to complaining about his bad luck with women (apparently they are all "such bitches"). And really, what woman doesn't want to date a nice fella with some urine strapped to his leg? Yes, I could choose to leave the line or even leave the Con altogether, but removing women's opportunities to prevent their victimization is an abhorrent excuse for a policy.

Why would these men feel so comfortable displaying such sophomoric, sexist behavior, particularly in front of a teenage girl? Because the culture at large presents this as acceptable and natural—even desirable. We live in a "rape culture" that defines women as objects of sexual conquest rather than as sexual agents. These aspects of society infiltrate Comic-Con to such a degree that the blogger who frames the Con as "one big Hollywood tease" probably doesn't recognize the sexist, gender-normative undertones of that metaphor. Likewise, when panelists discuss sexism in the industry, there is little patience for the topic. As noted at the blog Geeks Out, male attendees salivate over just about everything at the Con "unless it's about sexism. Unless it has even a whiff of feminism. Then, it's GAME OVER."

Notable examples of the intolerance for "lady topics" have occurred at the "Women Who Kick Ass" panels in recent years. Terms such as *white male privilege* and *destructive male culture* were employed by the likes of Danai Gurira and Michelle Rodriguez in 2013. Apparently, such discussion upset the "Hall H brohive" (as it's defined here). The female panelists' searing stories of sexism in the industry made many in the audience squirm and grumble sexist comments. One man, presumably suggesting a more apt title for the panel, shouted out, "Women who talk too much!" If audience members in Hall H would be so rude to a panel of smart and accomplished women in the fields and media they claim to love, just imagine what happens to the nonfamous females in attendance.

Feeling like a piece of meat at Comic-Con isn't always metaphorical. In 2013, zombie-related costumes proliferated, likely due to the popularity of AMC's *The Walking Dead*, Max Brook's *WWZ*, and popular games/comics such as *Lollipop Chainsaw*. One young woman's costume was particularly evocative: She wore a tight tank top and very short shorts, nothing unique in San Diego, but she'd used fake blood to write "Slutty Victim" across her top. The cursive claim called to mind the rape culture in which we reside, in which women supposedly "ask for it"; the media landscape in which women are reduced to stock types, including "ice queen" and "slutty victim"; *and* the Comic-Con culture, wherein some attendees feel entitled to ogle and, in some cases, sexually harass and/or assault women. Whether the woman I spotted meant her shirt as a feminist statement, I can't know. But, to me, it brought to mind the reclamation of the term *slut* (as with the SlutWalk movement) and the many activist events and organizations that seek to critique patriarchal perpetuations of the woman as a sex *object* without sexual *agency*.

While all attendees must jostle for position in the overcrowded and understocked convention hall, females have a harder time of it. It's not just the snaking lines for restrooms, it's the constant barrage of sexy, scantily clad female bodies. From billboards to movies, games, and comics, these images transmit the message that the female body is up for judgment and for sale. And, indeed, at Comic-Con, it is—one can pay for pictures with cosplayers and booth babes; buy miniature buxom vixens; and procure comics featuring everything from hypersexualized female villains to infantilized, animalized sexpots and girlish characters whose presentation borders on child pornography.

As writer and director Joss Whedon's body of work and various responses to it attest, there is no norm in place for a female hero, especially one who isn't sexed to the hilt. During a panel for comic publisher Dark Horse at the 2011 Comic-Con, Whedon complained that he had been coming to San Diego for 10 years but had yet to find a female hero statue he could purchase that didn't look like a porn star. When Whedon went on to describe the story of his career as depicting women who are not helpless, I was reminded of the Zombie Dice game I encountered on the exhibit floor in 2011. There were separate characters for action hero and girlfriend. When I asked the man demonstrating the game why the girlfriend couldn't be an action hero too, he said, "Oh, it gets worse: He has two brains and she only has one." He continued, "But it's OK because they save each other." Too bad the creator of this game didn't take a page from Whedon's book to create a woman with enough brains to save herself!

Alas, I may be waiting a while to see gender-equitable panels and a Con devoid of women treated as slutty victims, but until then, I will revel in the Con's more enjoyable aspects while keeping a critical eye on those areas in dire need of improvement. Who knows, maybe a Con in the near future will be the one where Whedon finds a nonpornified female hero statue!

## RECOMMENDED READING

Melissa McEwan. 2009. "Rape Culture 101." Retrieved January 28, 2015 (shakesville.com/2009/10/rape-culture-101.html). Defines and documents the extent to which rape culture pervades pop culture.

Angela McRobbie. 2004. "Post-feminism and Popular Culture." Pp. 255–264 in *Feminist Media Studies*, edited by Liesbet van Zoonen. Thousand Oaks, CA: Sage Publications. Characterizes the pop culture of the 1990s as a setback in feminism that has not yet been regained.

Laura Mulvey. 1973. "Visual Pleasure and Narrative Cinema," *Screen* 16(3): 6–18. This oft-cited film studies piece introduces the concept of the male gaze.

K. L. Pereira. 2006. "The Strange History of Wonder Woman." Retrieved January 28, 2015 (bitchmagazine.org/article/female -bonding). Explores the creation of the first female superhero to hit comics. See also Lillian S. Robinson's *Wonder Women: Feminisms and Superheroes* (Routledge, 2004).

John Scalzi. 2012. "Straight White Male: The Lowest Difficulty Setting There Is." Retrieved January 28, 2015 (whatever .scalzi.com). A *New York Times* best-selling author's humorous essay using role-playing games to look at privilege and intersectionality.

# TSP tie-in

This volume has covered a lot of ground—from fashion-following trots around the globe to standardized beauty ideals. Taken together, the essays demonstrate the value of a sociological analysis of a bounded cultural object. In particular, our authors detail the production of the material (and immaterial aspects) of culture as well as our consumption of them through participation and internalization of cultural ideals. Peeling back the layers of social activity helps us discover the influence of larger social forces and allows for a critical analysis of usually hidden stratifying processes and power hierarchies.

The Society Pages hosts many features that employ a cultural lens, including a few on a subject near and dear to us: food. As a cultural object, food is a daily part of our lives and an even more important part of our selves. This obsession can be seen in the explosion of food blogs written by self-proclaimed "foodies," seemingly endless dietary fads, and increasing attention to ethical consumption. Contributors to The Society Pages use their sociological imaginations not only to uncover ignored inequalities and relationships within the production and consumption of food but also to implore us to ask the most fundamental question, What *is* food?

In "Pink Slime and the Modern Jungle," Roundtable participants Michael Bell, Valentine Cadieux, Julie Guthman, and Marion Nestle use the public outrage over grocery store beef as a starting point to critique large systems of food production. The panel highlights how anxiety over food too often exists at the superficial level: The "yuck factor" determines what is considered good food worthy of consumption. If it reaches a tipping point, as in the case of pink slime, people who can afford to may seek alternative food sources. However, the turn to local or organic foods often occurs without addressing the systems through which the majority of food for the majority of people is produced or pressuring regulators or calling for industry transparency. A more serious focus that goes beyond "yuck" reveals the entire food economy's connections to issues of health, environment, labor, and politics—and people's responses to food.

In another example, Samira Kawash joined the Office Hours podcast to discuss her book *Candy: A Century of Panic and Pleasure.* In it, she traces the history of sweets in the

United States, revealing the complicated and ever-shifting relationship candy has had with "food" and the American diet. This includes celebrations of sugary treats as symbols of modern abundance and of the chocolate bar as a healthy, calorie-rich form of sustenance for soldiers, athletes, and the general populace in the golden age of candy consumption that surrounded WWII. Turning to the more recent era of mistrust, led by nutritionists and moral objectors, Kawash shows how candy has lately become a scapegoat for all manner of ailments, even as sugar-packed protein bars, flavored yogurts, and indulgent cereals remain "food." By going on such historical journeys, we see how multiple meanings can be attached to the same cultural object and how studying them helps reveal the dominant discourses and concerns of a time.

It seems that as we ask, What is food? we are also asking, Who are we?

—STEPHEN SUH AND KYLE GREEN

# 8

# burning man with katherine k. chen, s. megan heller, and jon stern

**MATT WRAY**

ach year around Labor Day, nearly 60,000 people gather to participate in Burning Man, an "experimental community" committed to art, creativity, and free expression. The festival began on a San Francisco beach in 1986 and has since moved to the Black Rock Desert, a vast alkali salt flat in northwestern Nevada. Here on "the playa," as the ancient seabed is called, participants construct the teeming Black Rock City. The pop-up utopia is built up from hundreds of individual "theme camps" (extended households or tribes), ranging in size from 5 to 500 individuals and organized around a common identity, concept, or practice.

Everywhere, there is art—performance art, installation art, body art, experiential and immersive art—scaled from the microscopic to the size of tractor trailers. Participants are encouraged to embrace, imbibe, and abide by the 10 principles of the event. These include the ideals of radical inclusion, self-expression, and self-reliance as well as an ethos of gift giving, immediacy, and leaving no trace. Some of the 10 principles (like *decommodification*, defined as resisting "the substitution of consumption for participatory experience") stand in sharp contrast to mainstream American values. Others, like radical self-reliance, lay at the core of the American dream.

Burning Man brings to mind a lot of preconceptions, but it also raises a lot of questions, from the sociological to the plain old curious. What is this event about? What purposes does it serve? Who is involved and why? And what does this festival say about art and expression in America? I brought together three of my fellow social scientists—all of whom have attended the event, think of themselves as "Burners," and have done research on Burning Man—to talk a bit about what these days in the desert mean to us and what larger social significance Burning Man might hold.

*Many Burners have adopted a "playa name," something like a public persona. Why is your playa name, if you have one, meaningful to you? How are alter egos socially significant?*

**Katherine Chen:** I don't have a playa name, but most Burners do. Asking about how someone has acquired a nickname can reveal insights into a person's biography, past and future. For example, "Chicken John" told me that he got his nickname as a youngster because when he got angry, his friends thought he looked like a chicken. Others pick names that they aspire to.

In general, playa names help people explore and develop new identities and roles—ones that may not be assigned by characteristics that people are born with (like race/ethnicity or gender, for instance). People may also change their playa names to reflect their growth. I think the phenomenon of playa names speaks partly to the

© Matt Wray, reprinted with permission.

constraints of society (not everyone wants to be known just as an employee of such-and-such organization or the relative of so-and-so) and partly to people's capacity for creativity and reinvention. Jon Stern has been working on this phenomenon at Burning Man and in the virtual-reality game world Second Life.

**Jon Stern:** I didn't have a playa name until my third year. That year I worked with Census and got gifted the names "Gadget" and "Gadget Fairy" by Black Rock City Census [a data-collection project undertaken at each year's festival]. However, the playa name I use mostly is "Wee Heavy." It's the name I use with the Black Rock Rangers (the volunteer safety and security team) and it has also become my handle in the PG&E (the perimeter, gate, and exodus) Department of the festival as well. Wee Heavy comes from the name of a particular beer from AleSmith Brewing in San Diego.

Even as my personal identity and appearance have shifted, my playa name has remained constant. For me, it's an important part of my identity, but I know that playa names often have various levels of meaning to the individual. Some long-time staff have playa names but still choose to use their given names (like Seth, the Exodus Manager who has been nicknamed "Blue Cross"), while departments that use radios require playa names or han-

© Matt Wray, reprinted with permission.

dles, and those handles become important signifiers of that person's particular identity.

**Matt Wray:** While I agree with Katherine and Wee Heavy about how playa names are used to help Burners create new identities—or remake old ones—I think that there are some other things going on as well. Like Jon's first playa names, I didn't really choose my playa name. Mine, "Burping Man," was given to me by my theme camp because I have the ability to belch loudly and to talk— whole paragraphs—at the same time. In most contexts, this questionable talent is met with disgust or, at best, mild amusement. On the playa, it has become central to my identity in a way I never anticipated or even asked for. Off playa, I'm a nice guy—I try to be civil to everyone I meet. But Burping Man is a bit of a rude asshole, a bit surly and always trying to provoke disgust. I've tried various times to retire this persona, but there is always protest. It's a role I'm practically required to play while I'm there. Rather than fight that war, I burp.

So you see, even in my alter ego, I'm somewhat constrained by community standards, habits, and expectations. It sounds ridiculous to say it, but being Burping Man has made me wonder how free any of us really are as individuals.

**Megan Heller:** Anthropologist Thomas Weisner has argued that human development is not a linear process—a person can develop along many possible pathways. I would add that these developmental pathways can multiply in environments that foster personal explorations—and where names are not fixed! The significance of a new playa name is that it allows a person to explore and develop an alternative possibility for the self—in terms of identity, of course, but also in terms of their comportment and skills. I have had many playa names over the years:

"Bunny" (because I was wearing bunny ears that day), "Chameleon" (because people often do not recognize me in various costumes), and "Ginger Snap" (because of my temper), but the playa name that most people know me by is "the Countess." I gave myself this name when I assumed management of the Black Rock City Census in 2004.

The Countess is a female version of the Count from *Sesame Street.* As the Countess, I count Burners: "One Burner, two Burners, three Burners, four . . . *muah ha ha ha ha!*" I have encouraged other members of the census team to assume mathematical names. "Equator," "Variance," and "Random" have followed the tradition.

As the Countess, I have assumed a great deal of responsibility (on and off the playa) for a very large, collaborative data-collection project called the Black Rock City Census. The experience has given me an opportunity to grow into that leadership role and learn new skills, including how to collaborate with researchers and volunteers from many parts of the globe and the Burning Man organization. Simultaneously, I express my femininity through this persona, using creative costuming and adopting a fiercely protective, motherly attitude toward my team. The Countess has given me a platform for learning and growth, as well as a recognizable position in the community.

© Matt Wray, reprinted with permission.

*Why might the demographics of the Burning Man population be of interest to researchers? For instance, there is a cultural trope that people who go to Burning Man are often marginalized individuals—outsiders in some way. Could the festival's annual census be used to measure this rather subjective characteristic of the population? Is there a single "modal demographic"—a specific Burner "type"—or are there many? What else does the census lab measure (or not measure)?*

**Chen:** People often have an idea of what they think the typical Burner is in terms of age or interests, but the census's convenience survey has revealed greater diversity than people might expect. One Burner compared Burning Man to the Internet—if you can think it, you can find someone else who is into it at Burning Man. As media images show, Burning Man does attract subcultures of persons who might be marginalized in their hometowns because of their appearance, interests, or ways of thinking. At the same time, people who do not appear marginal also attend Burning Man, perhaps because they are seeking a connection of some sort.

Given this, maybe the question should be more about how alienation (rather than marginalization) pushes people toward Burning Man. When I interviewed people about why they volunteered, putting in long hours of work, sometimes back-breaking labor, they cited reasons such as: They got more meaning out of their work for Burning Man than their paid work, they wanted to meet more people who were similar thinking, they wanted a new experience besides what they have gotten from work and family, etc. Maybe the census could measure how Burning Man alleviates (or fosters) alienation.

**Burping Man (Wray):** I'll leave the question about what types of people frequently show up at Burning Man to the Countess [Heller], who has a better handle on the census data than I do, but I've always been struck at how *little* the demographics of Burning Man reflect the diversity of the Bay Area or California more generally. While it is true that there is a wide array of subcultures represented at the event, there is much less racial diversity than you might expect. I attended for 14 consecutive years, from 1993 to 2006, and perhaps it has changed in more recent years, but the whiteness of Burning Man was striking. So I never thought of Burners as marginalized members of society. Quite the opposite: The event seemed to be pulling from the most privileged racial group.

I like Katherine's reframing of the question because I've always thought that perhaps Burners were drawn to the event as a way of dealing with unwanted privilege—a kind of potlatch ceremony where whites give up the excess they have accumulated over the year and try to re-distribute that to a larger community, as a way of unburdening themselves of both the excess and the guilt that comes with having been given too much. This is a very tribal dynamic at work: If you don't periodically burn off the abundant excess, tribal solidarity fails. I think this may be part of the symbolic significance of the event, whether or not most participants are aware of it. Does this interpretation make any sense to anyone else? Where is an anthropologist when you need one? Countess?

**Wee Heavy (Stern):** The demographics are difficult to pinpoint, but there are some patterns that are easy to discern. This is a diverse event, but the majority of participants remain white, and if I had to make a guess on the average age, I'd say late thirties. While it is indeed a very white event, the class tiers that exist within this white group of people are many. The class diversity stems in some part due to the differences that exist between the rich participant groups from the Silicon Valley and the less-well-off groups that staff event services.

**Countess (Heller):** As an anthropologist, I appreciate Matt's analysis of the potlatch and Katherine's point about alienation. Perhaps there might be a way to measure alienation—or, the term I prefer: *dislocation*. Any ideas from readers about how to measure this would be appreciated.

On this question of the demographics, I'd rather not report modal statistics on demographic variables. I would rather not feed into people's desires to characterize, label, and stereotype others by reducing the complexity of an entire population down to a single number. I prefer to display entire distributions. Certainly the Black Rock City Census data show that there are a lot of people in their thirties and a lot of white people at Burning Man, but there is a great deal of diversity as well. Diversity tends to be overlooked when researchers focus on the center of a distribution.

For example, the majority of burners identify as heterosexual, but this does not negate the fact that other sexual orientations are quite acceptable and visible at Burning Man. Many find that Black Rock City is a very safe place to come out of the closet and experiment with their sexuality. Some minorities and subcultural groups may find Burning Man to be a tolerant place; others may not. The main point of the census, in my mind, is to explore this diversity and share our findings with the Burning Man community and the press.

The census is no longer using just a convenience sample. In 2012, we successfully instituted a random sample, which we conducted at the main entrance gate. We are now using that representative data to adjust the results of last year's paper form and the online survey we conducted after the event. In 2013, we will focus our efforts on the random sample and the online survey only. We will no longer be using the paper form.

*Burning Man sometimes gets portrayed as little more than a giant rave—a psychedelic party on the playa. It is like a party in many ways, but those of us who go know that the label doesn't begin to capture the full experience. What larger phenomena does Burning Man represent in your research? In other words, how do you categorize the event and why should we take it seriously?*

**Chen:** People often forget that Burning Man arises from larger society. Although people may see Burning Man as an escape from society, the festival is still informed by society; people bring their habits, customs, and ideas with them. In these ways, Burning Man reflects society.

At the same time, the festival's internal principles, some of which run counter to societal norms, encourage creative transformations of seemingly mundane, everyday actions. Burning Man principles that urge participation, self-expression, and community can help transform the meaning of picking up litter under "Leave No Trace," for instance. Burning Man also enables people to develop rituals, such as grieving for a departed loved one (see Lee Gilmore and Sarah Pike's respective work, for instance) or biking en masse alongside one's compatriots (see Wendy Clupper's analysis of Critical Tits, the female bike parade), that aren't readily available in society at large.

For me, the most fascinating aspect of Burning Man is how it regularly organizes creative, large-scale output. On the one hand, you don't want to underorganize or provide too little support and coordination for people's efforts, such that the event falls apart. On the other hand, you don't want to overorganize, or have excessive organization that relies on coercion to encourage people to carry out actions. Most people are familiar with the latter via their experiences with bureaucracies at work, for instance, and they don't want to repeat those experiences. Nor do they want a routinized output like what Disney produces. My book *Enabling Creative Chaos: The Organization Behind the Burning Man Event* and other publications address how to avoid these excesses and explore other issues, like how do you inspire people to take unfamiliar action?

One promising area of research is how Burning Man's principles and activities have spread around the world in the form of regionals and Burning Man–inspired events, organizations, and voluntary associations. Although such offshoots will retain some elements of Burning Man, the practices are likely to change meaning in local contexts. If so, researchers could study: How are these expressed and how might they feed back into Burning Man, possibly reinvigorating Burning Man? In addition, what's the impact of Burning Man upon larger society? How is Burning Man building social capital and fostering community resilience?

**Burping Man (Wray):** I really like Katherine's questions about the spreading influence of Burning Man. It would make an interesting case study in the process of global cultural diffusion, especially since it has a clear start date.

© Matt Wray, reprinted with permission.

In terms of how I label the event, I have always found it useful and instructive to view it through the historical lens of American experiments with utopian, intentional communities. These have a long, fascinating, and mostly unknown history, since you're not likely to see it in most high-school textbooks. Utopian communitarianism involves a group of people choosing to set themselves apart in a new place in order to make a better world according to visions and principles they share. This has most often arisen from religious impulses—the Puritans are an early example of Americans doing this, as are the

Mormons—but there have also been secular versions, a large number of which ended up in California (see Robert Hine's *California's Utopian Colonies*), which is where Burning Man originated in 1986.

What's distinctive about Burning Man is that it is a *temporary* intentional community. It's more like a family reunion or a bluegrass festival than it is like a settlement of true believers. And I'm very interested in this temporary aspect of the event because I think that is a key ingredient in its special sauce. It's part of what has made the event so enormously successful—far more successful, in many ways, than any of its historical forbears, most of which failed spectacularly within a few years. I think future researchers might explore this element of the event's organization—its temporal dimension—quite fruitfully. Is ephemerality part of its success? Is impermanence what makes it sustainable?

**Wee Heavy (Stern):** I like to think of Burning Man as a social experiment, an artistic gathering, and an event that seems simple on the surface but belies a complex machine underneath. My research focuses on identity, and Burning Man is a fertile ground for exploration of identity. In the process of doing my own research, I found myself comfortable enough to come out of the closet, which I did in June 2011. I came out gender queer (meaning I'm both a man and a woman and either at the same time) because I found a group of people who supported me for who I am, and I knew even if I lost everyone else in my life, I'd still have them.

Sure, on the surface Burning Man seems like a big party, but most things seem simple if we only take a look at the surface. If we peel back layers from the surface, we can see the intense level of infrastructure that exists supporting the participant's ability to party. Reinforcing Katherine's points, the organization that brings about the creativity at the event is well maintained and staffed by an array of talented volunteers who make the event occur. We can see the gift economy thriving in the capacity of volunteers who work tirelessly in many departments to make the entire city function as it should.

**Countess (Heller):** I describe Burning Man as a playground. The focus of my research is adult play and transformation. In the United States, children's play is considered important and valuable, if not essential, to a child's healthy development. But at Burning Man, adult play is considered important; it is the central point of the event. The question posed here shows a cultural prejudice against adult play and adult play spaces, such as raves and parties, where adults are allowed to experience the transformative potential of play. In my research, I see opportunities to play freely, without ordinary social constraints, as potentially benefiting an adult as they develop over time. On the playa, just as on a playground, a person may discover or invent possibilities that might seem impossible in ordinary cultural contexts. I take the Burning Man event seriously as a playground to explore human potentials and to develop cultural practices that promote individual well-being and strengthen ties of interpersonal relatedness.

*Burning Man is many different things to many different people. But at the center of the experience is a commitment to free expression and creativity. This puts the event squarely in the arena of "culture," as most people understand the word. Yet this conventional view of culture is pretty narrow. Social scientists use the word more broadly, encompassing how people in groups organize their worlds. What broad aspects of culture do you see operating at Burning Man?*

**Chen:** Experiences at Burning Man can enlarge people's ways of seeing, being, interacting, and thinking. A big one for me is the expansion of the organizing tool kit. Once people figure out that they don't have to wait for institutions to organize things for them, they can take action and produce projects that can meet or even exceed people's expectations. Of course, we're talking about people who have the resources and inclination to undertake projects. (In other words, I don't think that this can necessarily substitute for the state or other societal arrangements—they can be complementary.)

Another aspect is that Burning Man can help people examine taken-for-granted beliefs. In everyday life, people often accept phenomena such as poverty, inequality, racism, sexism, environmental degradation, and other social issues as "the way that the world works." At Burning Man, these issues don't go away, but people can start to imagine other possibilities and actions that they can take to address these. Although these actions may initially be small scale, they may add up to something larger. In other words, Burning Man can cultivate what social scientists call reflexivity. For example, Burners will ask what does it mean to be inclusive? What if someone does something harmful or distasteful to the community? Are we still obligated to include that person? How can we encourage people to reduce waste and recycle? Can we do this in a fun way? How do we prod transgressors to alter their ways? These are all dilemmas that people will have to contend with no matter where they are, from a small village to the World Wide Web.

**Burping Man (Wray):** In a recent essay, I try to convince readers that Burning Man makes an interesting case study for cultural sociologists. I talk about the search for meaning that we all experience and how that search always draws from—and contributes to—shared representations of the world. Like Katherine, I find that a lot of Burners are innovators. They don't wait for society to present solutions to their problems. . . . Instead, they imagine new solutions. Sometimes—a great deal of the time, if I'm honest—this takes the form of mockery and satire: Let's dispense with this social problem by making fun of the people who think it is a problem. So you have a great deal of playa humor aimed at bureaucratic society; the failures of government and religion; and at people whose views of sex, gender, and drugs—to take just a few examples—seem puritanical, phobic, and punitive to Burners.

I like this DIY/steampunk/anarchic spirit hovering over the event. It's a fierce, guardian spirit that resists turning a cultural innovation into just another commodity. It insists that these innovations be given as gifts. That really feeds me, because so much of what American culture offers up for consumption is so bland and conformist, even as it revels in its own brand of cool iconoclasm (see Frank's *The Conquest of Cool*). I don't dislike commodified American culture because I'm a snob. I dislike it because it makes me feel dead inside. And whenever I'm

© Matt Wray, reprinted with permission.

on the playa, I know I'm not alone in feeling that way. And that makes me feel connected to others, which is pretty much what everyone needs to feel in order to be happy. So this aspect of the culture of Burning Man, which feels inclusive to those of us who feel excluded—or to use Katherine's term, *alienated*—by American culture, this aspect needs to be better understood by social scientists.

**Wee Heavy (Stern):** Culture is indeed a multifaceted concept. . . . Some cultural aspects of Burning Man include ritual, micro-level interaction, the pervasiveness of the 10 principles, the transmission of information, and the art we don't see as art. The event itself is a ritual, but it is also made up of many smaller rituals that have varying levels of importance for a given participant or the city as a whole. For many, even the journey to the event is a major part of their ritual. . . .

Micro-level interactions are very important to the overall atmosphere and culture of TTITD—That Thing in the Desert, as Burning Man is sometimes called. As a person who lives out—openly queer—my interactions with strangers in the default world can range from nice and cordial to people staring at me, taking pictures without my permission, and making rude comments. Interactions on playa tend to be uniformly cordial, polite, and respectful, even if they only last a few seconds. This plays off of Katherine's points about what people normally take for granted. While the event is only a week long, I've been extending my time on playa both for my own enjoyment and to conduct more fieldwork with staff pre- and postevent. Acclimating to the playa isn't simply something that takes place physically. It also involves acculturating and becoming part of the social atmosphere that exists around us.

**Countess (Heller):** I see the Burning Man event as an antidote to the widespread experience of dislocation, the condition in which most of us find ourselves, shorn of culture and individual identity in a globalized world in which people's needs are subordinate to the market. Burning Man is an opportunity to be *relocated*, to experience a potential home where people's needs are valued . . . and people are encouraged to bring creative cultural practices and identities to share with others. To experience a real sense of home, even for only one week . . . and to set one's roots deep in that ground, is to be given a sense of pride and belonging that can be . . . taken with you wherever you roam.

## PARTICIPANT PROFILES

**Katherine K. Chen** is in the department of sociology at the City College of New York and the Graduate Center, CUNY. She is the author of *Enabling Creative Chaos: The Organization Behind the Burning Man Event* (University of Chicago Press, 2009).

**S. Megan Heller** (the Countess) is an anthropologist and an expert on play. She is currently lecturing at the University of California, Los Angeles. Applying a neuroanthropological approach to her mixed-methods research, Heller has identified an ethos of play at Burning Man that seems to have significant effects on behavioral and cultural patterns.

**Jon Stern** (Wee Heavy) is a sociologist whose interest lies in identity and alternative space. They have been researching Burning Man since 2010. Jon's queer identity and deep involvement with both the Black Rock Rangers (fourth year) and BRC Perimeter Gate and Exodus (third year) shape their view of identity at Burning Man.

**Matt Wray** (Burping Man) is in the sociology department at Temple University and is the editor of *Cultural Sociology: An Introductory Reader* (W. W. Norton, 2012). He has been writing about Burning Man since 1995.

# culture as ways
# of life: communities
# and lifestyles

9

# together alone with eric klinenberg

**ARTURO BAIOCCHI AND STEPHEN SUH**

n his book *Going Solo: The Extraordinary Rise and Surprising Appeal of Living Alone*, sociologist Eric Klinenberg explains that in 1950, just 4 million Americans (roughly 9 percent of the adult population) lived alone. Today, about 33 million Americans live alone (according to the 2011 Census). The shift is most noticeable in a number of mid- to large-size cities in which 40 to 50 percent of all households are occupied by a single resident.

Klinenberg posits that this remarkable transformation in living patterns is, in part, explained by more widespread prosperity, though this has been mostly limited to countries with strong welfare programs: "When you have generous welfare states that provide subsidized housing and guaranteed access to health care, home care, and a social insurance (what we call Social Security in the United States), it makes it much easier for people to have domestic independence."

"[Another] big driver of living alone is women's independence and also their capacity to control their own lives, to control their own bodies." Klinenberg goes on to point out that delays in marriage and family life typically accompany these new forms of female independence; there are fewer economic and social penalties that would have adversely affected single women in the past. In the United States, women account for more single-resident households than do men (about 18 million compared to about 14 million), while a country like Saudi Arabia may have an abundance of affluence and prosperity but very few people actually living alone.

At the core of the "going solo" trend is a wider *cultural shift*, especially in the United States, where it is no longer a deeply socially stigmatized act. Not only has it become more socially acceptable to live alone, members of the younger generations are leading this charge:

> There's this whole new part of life where people are living by themselves and experiencing all kinds of things that previous generations did not. And again, let me put this in perspective for you, in 1950 only 1 percent of young adults under the age of 30 lived alone, today 11 percent do—from 500,000 in 1950 to more than 5 million in 2010. This in an incredible change. And I know that these days there's a lot of concern about the "boomerang generation" and this idea that the labor

market has been so bad for young people that it's impossible for them to launch into the world—that they leave their parents' home and come crashing back into the basement. Well, that's true—there are more young adults living with their families than in many decades, but at the same time there are another set of young adults who are doing well and getting places of their own, paying a premium for it. In fact, from the recession in 2008 to today the proportion of young adults living alone dropped only 1 percent, from 12 percent to 11 percent, so this is still a big phenomenon.

Klinenberg establishes a few reasons as to why these changes have occurred:

There's a lot of pressure on the individual these days to come up with a way to live, but the conventional, traditional structures that oriented us in life have broken up in many ways. That's true for young people, but it's true for all of us because the family has changed so much. And again, that puts a lot of pressure on individuals. So, what I believe now is that young people, young adults have gotten concerned that employers will not make lifetime career commitments to them; the idea that you would have a job for 40 years is silly for most people. Maybe there's some academics who can still get that, but for most of the population you can't. People have grown up these days in the midst of the divorce revolution, and they don't believe that getting married is the key to lifetime security. They're skeptical that marriages will work out, and in a good percentage of cases they don't. And so, young adults feel the need to invest more and more time and energy into themselves: They get more education, they build their networks, they move from job to job trying to find the thing that fits well, getting the right kind of experience. And interestingly, you know, in people's late twenties and early thirties, they feel that that's precisely not the time to get married and tie themselves down to another person or to a lifestyle. That's why rates of marriage have decreased and the age of first marriage has gone up so high. In many American cities now the age of first marriage is over 30. So, this I think is a very difficult thing. It suggests that there's a lot of anxiety and insecurity out there. But perhaps living alone is a productive way to deal with that.

Moreover, Klinenberg argues that living alone has become a key life course stage for many young adults. One such reason for this is that it introduces them to the concept of freedom:

Why else do [young people] want it? Because when you live alone as a young person you have the freedom to do what you want to do when you want to do it. You have the time to invest in yourself. You can be very flexible; you can experiment. Michael Rosenfeld has written an entire book called *The Age of Independence* about the kind of sexual experiments that people have, mostly marrying across racial and ethnic lines, that are just more difficult if you are living with people who are judging you (like your family) all the time. So this is very consequential stuff. I would argue that for young people at a time when the age of marriage is so high, getting your own apartment is the way to become an adult. For a lot of affluent young people—successful, professional young people—living alone is the key part of the transition to adulthood.

By living alone, young adults can also learn skills that may become useful during later stages of their lives, such as marriage:

I'll say something else, which is that a lot of young people say that by living alone they gained a set of skills for living that served them quite well in marriages. And, in fact, we know that people who delay getting married are more likely to marry successfully and to avoid divorce than people who marry very young. This is something we need to understand. It's not as if you make a vow to live alone forever because living alone doesn't require that. Instead, you make a decision to try it and to experience it. And I should be clear about this; I believe that you cannot understand the rise of living alone outside of the concept of choice.

Klinenberg ascertains that the rise in living alone cannot be comprehended completely without acknowledging the fact that it is a lifestyle that people are increasingly *choosing* to adopt. This choice, however, is shaped by sociocultural factors that make the act of living alone more appealing. Furthermore, Klinenberg asserts that "living alone, being alone, and feeling lonely are three dramatically different things":

> The majority of Americans who live alone these days are between the age of 35 and 65; they're middle-aged adults—about 16 million people. Typically, they have been married before or at least they've lived with someone else. And they say with great frequency that there is nothing lonelier than living with the wrong person; there's nothing lonelier than being in the wrong marriage. They say the people in their lives worry about how lonely they'll be because they're living alone, but in fact when they feel lonely while going solo, that loneliness is kind of a physiological cue that they should get out into the world and reconnect with people, be active, do things. It's not always easy to do that, and some people have real problems with loneliness and depression, but often they can. When you're married, you're lying down next to someone in bed at night and you feel isolated and lonely. That is a profound and difficult feeling, a very difficult one. And it's not clear what the cue is. . . .
>
> I'm not denying that there are benefits to good marriages. I think there are and I'm voting with my feet on that one. But I also think it's irresponsible to tell people to stay in bad mar-

riages or to get married early because we know that those things could be really bad for you.

In a society still oriented toward "typical" family structures, Klinenberg admits that there remain limitations to living alone:

People who live alone are on average more likely to spend time with friends and neighbors and even to volunteer in civic organizations than people who are married. And that's true for young adults, but it's also true for older people who live alone. A really nice research project by the sociologists Benjamin Cornwell and Ed Laumann showed that. But, that said, it needs to be acknowledged that for many people living alone can lead to isolation and loneliness. And if you are isolated or if you don't have a big support network, if you get very sick with something difficult that requires long-term care and you don't have family or friends who are immediately available to help you with those everyday difficulties it can be a very challenging situation. I don't think that we should be shy about this. In fact I believe that we need to have more conversations publicly about the challenges of providing care for people who live alone and really need support and assistance. I don't believe that we have that conversation very effectively or productively when we talk about things like "bowling alone" or when we complain about the extent to which our society has fallen apart. That turns into kind of this generalized lament rather than a very specific concern. But I think that we could identify the people and the places where isolation is really risky and dangerous and do far more to target them with services and care.

Klinenberg, nonetheless, is steadfast in his belief that "going solo" is a phenomenon that is here to stay. Further, while others may wax poetic about the supposed neighborliness of the 1950s and 1960s, Klinenberg points out that this cultural nostalgia is largely unfounded:

So, that's an idea that comes with a story that goes like this, "Once upon a time we lived in a world in which there were stronger communities, closer friendships, more successful and better marriages, safer streets, less loneliness, happier people. Once upon a time we lived in that world and since that time has ended we have fallen into a terrible world of atomization and isolation and sadness. We are despondent; we are disconnected from each other." Surely, you recognize that narrative. It is part of almost all our conversations about what happens in the modern world.

Well, what I discovered doing research on this book is that, in fact, nothing could be further from the truth. First of all, it turns out that golden age never really existed. Think for a minute about the TV show *Mad Men*, if you will. That lands us right back into that golden age of American communities and perfect marriages. Think about the loneliness, and the pain, and the isolation that exists in the Draper family household and in many of the families that you see in that TV show. In a way, that show is all about the disconnection of highly connected people during this golden age.

Rather, Klinenberg argues that the increase in living alone is a distinct cultural product of our increasingly competitive and frenetic social world, and it's not something we can simply "moralize . . . out of existence." Looking at countries in Europe, Asia, and South America as models, Klinenberg concludes that new public policies like the restructuring and rezoning of suburban areas and the creation of better public transit and more accessible commercial areas will better support this change: "There's every reason to believe that this is a fundamental change in the modern world that is here to stay. And in my view, it's folly to persuade people that this is a bad idea and to scare people off from all the dangers of doing this. We have to come to terms with the social fact that this is who we are and this is what we ought to do."

## PARTICIPANT PROFILE

**Eric Klinenberg** is a sociologist and the director of the Institute for Public Knowledge at New York University. A prolific author and public scholar, he is the editor of the journal *Public Culture*.

# deep play and flying rats with colin jerolmack

**KYLE GREEN**

"Pigeons are believed to be the first domesticated bird and perhaps one of the first domesticated animals—between five and ten thousand years ago. There's a lot of things they're useful for," says Colin Jerolmack, author of *The Global Pigeon*. He goes on to explain that pigeons were once prized for their meat and eggs, their guano (which made an excellent fertilizer), and their famed homing ability. Now, when cheaper, fatter chickens have replaced them at the dinner table, nitrogen has ousted guano as the world's preferred fertilizer, and all manner of technology has made the flying missive obsolete, they are essentially urban rats of hundreds of breeds. "So what you have is birds who actually thrive around people in the built environment—better than they ever did in their native habitat. They're thriving, but they're kind of 'historical detritus.'" And now, Jerolmack asserts, pigeons confront us as nuisances, adding a chaotic, "dirty" element to the pristine, manicured presentations of nature modern urbanites prefer. "They trespass in places defined for humans only."

The Society Pages talked to Jerolmack about how he came to lavish so much scholarly attention on an animal most people seem happy to shoo away.

**Kyle Green:** I'll start with the obvious question, "Why pigeons?"

**Colin Jerolmack:** When I was a very early grad student, I think in my second year of grad school, I took Mitchell Duneier's ethnography class at the City University of New York. We had to pick a project. I knew I was vaguely interested in public space, [so] I focused on a couple of parks in Greenwich Village. . . . I thought looking at a space that was going to be renovated [would] give me an opportunity to see how people use public space, what their dreams and hopes for it are. Whose vision wins out, who loses, who's seen as legitimate stakeholders? And so I started hanging out in a lot of these parks and going to community board meetings and talking to block associations and everyday visitors.

One of the things that I really hadn't anticipated was that a major talking point, point of concern . . . was pigeons, particularly in a place called Father Demo Square, which is quite small (less than a tenth of an acre), yet has hundreds of pigeons. [P]eople feed them regularly. [But] . . . the city was cracking down on pigeon feeding and issuing nuisance citations. And when I was talking to a lot of people about problems with the park, many complained about pigeons and homeless people the same way. They would say: If we could get rid of these pigeons and these homeless people, wouldn't these be great public spaces? There was this connection between pigeons and homeless and this sense that pigeons were dirty and filthy and somehow symbolize disorder.

As I started writing up some papers about these urban spaces for the ethnography class, I said, I can't really write about these spaces and how people experience them if I don't write about pigeons. So that's kind of how it started. . . . What made me decide to move forward with an entire project about pigeons was paying more attention to [them]—I lived in Bushwick, Brooklyn, at the time—and from my rooftop I would see six or seven stocks of pigeons, hundreds of them in each stock, circling. And I knew that these were bred by people. I knew about this working-class kind of male subculture, because it has a long history in New York. . . . And so I, out of curiosity, started to get to know [breeders]. Once

I realized there was this really fascinating story both about how the men experience the urban ecology through their birds and how this was traditionally an ethnic white practice (passed on to Puerto Ricans and blacks as the neighborhoods changed over), that's when I thought there was a lot I could do.

**Green:** Your book is organized into three sections: the pedestrian pigeon, the totemic pigeon, and the professional racing pigeon. In the third, you followed two rather different racing communities. Who are these guys in the Bronx who first captured your curiosity?

**Jerolmack:** The guys I talked about in the totemic pigeon portion of the book, they're not racing pigeons. They basically just breed [rooftop fliers] and train them to fly in tight-knit stocks . . . like a swarm of bees, if you will. It's the pleasure of training the birds to fly as a unit and, if they're lucky, they catch other people's pigeons, their stocks mix. . . . But pigeon racing . . . the idea here is to use the homing ability of pigeons. You can take them to a place they've never been and through their ability to sense electromagnetic radiation, see ultraviolet light, and use the sun as a compass . . . they can find their way home.

The idea here, then, is that . . . in the Bronx these men can put their pigeons on a truck and the truck can drive to Virginia. Then the pigeons can fly home four to five hundred miles and generally do it one day, a single day. [The winner is] the fastest pigeon measured by yards per minute (its velocity). So there's a measurement from the starting point to each racer's coop, where the birds are released. Everyone has exact GPS measurements.

To race in the club [I studied], you have to be within the borders of the Bronx. This necessarily makes it a parochial club. . . . Men have grown up and stayed in the neighborhood, and, in most instances, their fathers and even grandfathers were members of this club. . . . Generally it's men and almost all of them are working class, although they tend to be a little bit higher economic status than the rooftop fliers. . . . Pigeon racers have to train the birds every morning, drive them 50 to 100 miles away, which costs a lot of gas money. There are race entry fees and whatever, it costs more money. Generally the modal (or "typical") pigeon racer has retired from a city job (sanitation, policeman, fireman); they're blue-collar union people. Like the rooftop guys, [it's] a variety of ethnicities, older people, ethnic white, but there also were a number of Hispanic and African American men involved.

Generally they gather at the club, hang out, drink coffee, and watch the Yankees if there's a game on. Then they pack their birds in a truck and it drives off to Ohio, Virginia—wherever the race start is. The next day, the men wait on their rooftops for the birds to come home. When the birds fly home, their time is clocked when they come into the coop [because] there's an electronic band on their leg that is scanned by an electronic clock. . . . So sometimes when pigeons come home, they sit on the roof or fly around for a while. The guys can lose valuable time, so they wait on the rooftop and devise all sorts of strategies to bring the birds home [and into the coop]. They may bring out their mate. . . . They have various strategies. And then they bring their clocks back down to the club and see who won.

**Green:** So pigeon racing requires large amounts of time, at least some money, and what seems like a good amount of emotional energy. What is the seduction or appeal?

**Jerolmack:** You know, that's the question I struggled to answer. The things I think immediately spring to mind are competition and money. People like to win, people like to compete . . . and there is some money laid out for bets [and prizes]. But what I try to argue in the book is that it cannot be reduced to competition or money. Most men wager very little money and most men break even at best. The goal is not to be in the red by the end of the racing season, not really to clean up. And so I really tried to go deeper into what is it that compels these people, and this what I love about ethnography, the only way you can really discover this is to be there and participate in it.

And so what I argue is that pigeon racing offers an opportunity to really engage, to personally invest and engage in nature vs. nurture. So you take these birds, you breed them, and then you train them. So what all this is about is trying to control nature, to get the perfect breed and then through training . . . [to] bring the birds home quicker. . . . You try to unlock the secrets of nature and use them to your advantage.

But on the other hand, there's all sorts of elements that [racers] can't control. Once the birds are in the air, as one guy said to me, "They're in God's hands." There's all sorts of things you can't control . . . so you kind of open yourself up to the vicissitudes of nature. When your bird comes home, it's kind of this triumph over nature. . . . [E]very time it comes home, it really is kind of as magical as it seems to the person who doesn't know a lot about pigeons. When [the racer] sees their bird come over the horizon, even if the bird doesn't have a chance for first place any more, their mouth gets dry, they start shaking, the adrenaline is rushing. And when the bird comes home there's this sense that they did it. They beat the odds; they triumphed over nature.

**Green:** So am I right that the men you met in the Bronx didn't see pigeon racing as a way to enjoy nature but as a triumph over or struggle against it?

**Jerolmack:** That is a fair characterization. . . . When I first started hanging out with these guys who fly pigeons, my romantic idea was that this was their cabin on Walden Pond, their escape from the concrete jungle, their opportunity to bond with nature. What I found instead [were] men, men who in general had no other interest in nature. They didn't camp; they weren't interested in forming relationships with nature more generally. They didn't see it as an escape. It was more that they went to the rooftop with little bits of nature's raw material and delighted in their ability to sculpt it according to their own whims. But what I will say—this is important about ethnography— I didn't come up with this argument . . . by the men telling me "I like to triumph over nature." Rather, it came from me observing the way they talked about pigeon flying and what they actually did.

For instance, I talked about how the men obsessed over all types of strategies . . . trying to unlock the secret of genetics or weather predictions . . . ways that they would try to sort of wish for a better outcome. And if their bird came home though a storm? That was about as exciting as it gets. . . . That's what led me to this argument. Very few of the guys said, "I like controlling nature," . . . but it was what came out of me observing their more natural conversations and their reactions to seeing their birds come home.

**Green:** Let's go to South Africa now. What is the Million Dollar Pigeon Race?

**Jerolmack:** So the Million Dollar Pigeon Race is a race where the winner gets, when I last checked, $200,000. The second place winner gets $120,000 and so on down the line. The total payout is a million. . . . I went to the Million Dollar Pigeon Race in Sun City (the South African equivalent of Las Vegas) because the guys in the Bronx were talking about it and it's the biggest of the one-loft races. A lot of the guys in the [Bronx] club sort of saw [the Million Dollar Race] as the antithesis of the "craft": . . . You send your bird there and somebody else raises it, somebody else trains it, and when it flies "home" you aren't up on the rooftop corralling it in. . . . You've outsourced it to somebody else.

People from around the world, from 28 countries sent pigeons. . . . If I wanted to, there are people who will sell shares of a bird. . . . So Sun City brings all sorts of people who are not pigeon racers. Just like the Kentucky Derby, you can bet on a pigeon.

It was bizarre after waiting on the rooftop with the guys from the Bronx. In South Africa, we all sat in a stadium arena and there was this Jumbotron. . . . You're not allowed to be at the pigeon loft to watch, because it may scare the birds coming in. And so we basically sit there in an arena, thousands of us, waiting for the pigeons to come home on a video screen. Everybody's put money down. When the pigeon comes down, they walk across the threshold and it comes up on the video screen who the winner was.

. . . [T]he race only takes one day. . . . Again it was a big commercial affair; in the stadium they had all sorts of vendors selling all sorts of pigeon magazines or Million Dollar Pigeon Race gear. There was a restaurant set up so you could by food. . . . [P]eople hung out with other pigeon fanciers and they had guest speakers. People who were famous in the pigeon world talked about their techniques. They had a band entertaining people. But then, about two to three hours before the birds might come in, it really started to fill up. You never know: If the wind is to their back, maybe the pigeons will come home really quickly.

**Green:** Writing about the Million Dollar Pigeon Race, you drew on the writings of the famous anthropologist Clifford Geertz to talk how the event serves "as a story society tells about itself." What does his essay about "deep play" and Balinese cockfighting have to do with pigeon racers?

**Jerolmack:** Geertz shows how . . . there are all sorts of rules about who you can fight against and who you can bet for or against. These reflect the social hierarchy of society. . . . I find that [observation] useful. . . . There's all sorts of things that can be said to be cultural representations of a society. So the question here is: What does the Million Dollar Pigeon Race tell us about South African society and globalization?

. . . What I found really compelling was that in South Africa, this is a country still coming out of the shadow of apartheid and looking for ways to tell itself and everyone else that it is a diverse, democratic, and color-blind society. . . . The men [I met at the Million Dollar Race] who self-identified as "Colored" or "Black"* told me . . . they could recall an era where, of course, they were not free, under apartheid, but they'd raise pigeons back then. And so they were very insulted that there were separate clubs for whites; even if they had the best birds in their club, they were never able to prove they were the best in South Africa. . . . Through the Million Dollar Pigeon Race, they very clearly narrated this as, "Here I can come now, and I can go up against anyone in the world and . . . prove that I am the best of the best." For them there was an opportunity to recognize that, although there were still racial barriers and discrimination in South Africa . . . a meritocracy had actually flourished in the Million Dollar Pigeon Race. . . .

The organizers of the race didn't explicitly talk about apartheid at all, but they repeatedly emphasized the equality of the race, the equal opportunity, that this is a true meritocracy. That anyone has a chance to beat anyone. That people from around the world, no matter their station in life, have the opportunity to come and compete here.

This also plays out in another way. . . . Though you pretty much have to have a fair amount of money to go in

*South African respondents capitalized their racial categories.

this race, there are some relatively blue-collar people who may put in one bird. So they'll put in a thousand dollars, in the same way you might enter Powerball, right? Put in a little bit of money, very little chance to win, but you have a chance. I'd meet these blue-collar guy who would say, "You know, the Queen of England has pigeons in this race," which is true.... And so that was very powerful to people, right? So very much there was this really strong feeling of egalitarianism and meritocracy that, on one hand, I argue really sort of rang true and was deeply meaningful in South Africa, given the legacy of apartheid. But on the other hand, it very much rings with the sort of neoliberal idea of globalization and a flat world. People said, "Now we've broken down the barriers and people can compete against everybody. Everybody has an equal shot." There is a sort of feel-good story about globalization and how it levels the playing field.

**Green:** Before we were talking about that underlying tension in the relationship between the social and natural or the urban and the wild. Is this different in the Bronx versus in South Africa, in the big-money races?

**Jerolmack:** I play on the tension between the Bronx Club and the Million Dollar Pigeon Race. [In the Bronx], the idea is that you hope to triumph over nature. . . . So you actually have to make yourself vulnerable to being taken in and overwhelmed by nature. And then when you win, you feel that you've taken steps through the craft to kind of unlock the secrets of nature.

. . . [I]n South Africa there's no room for idiosyncrasy; there's one way to do it—whatever the veterinarians and the peer-reviewed literature say is the best way. And so it's very much scientific; it's very much the triumph of science over magic, if you will. It is the classic Weberian story of disenchantment . . . through the division of labor.

**Green:** To conclude our discussion, I wonder, what did the research project teach you about the discipline and how we actually go about studying the social world?

**Jerolmack:** [S]ociology, I'm happy to say, is a very diverse, open discipline. . . . My job [is to] demonstrate that relating to animals teaches us something about the traditional things that we scholars care about: community, identity, race, gender, class.

. . . [M]y goal has always been to . . . show how our relationships with animals actually organize and shape our relationships with other people. [Now] I'm researching fracking and how it's influencing communities in rural Pennsylvania, but it's related to this broader interest [in] how much the nonhuman (whether that means the built environment or the natural environment or animals) is actually the sort of scaffolding that organizes society.

## PARTICIPANT PROFILE

**Colin Jerolmack** is an environmental sociologist at New York University. He is the author of *The Global Pigeon* (University of Chicago Press, 2013).

# coded chaos and anonymous with gabriella coleman

**KYLE GREEN**

The word *anonymous* has come to mean more than a solitary, unknown person. Now it gets capitalized—Anonymous—and it's recognized as a loosely connected collective of hackers, activists, and Internet trolls. Together, this disparate group is affecting global politics, influencing offline activism, and becoming a legitimate news source. The Guy Fawkes masks its adherents use as an online symbol and a real-life mask are well known, associated with a sort of clandestine Robin Hood movement to, ironically, unmask the murky doings of government, wealth, and corporations. The Society Pages turned to Gabriella Coleman, author of *Coding Freedom: The Ethics and Aesthetics of Hacking*, for more insight into the activism of Anonymous, how people make use of the online space as well as how the group is portrayed in the media and even scapegoated by governments.

**Kyle Green:** In your research, you discuss a number of Internet-based collectives, including 4chan and Anonymous. What is Anonymous and what does it have to do with a website like 4chan?

**Gabriella Coleman:** Anonymous is many different things. Currently it's most famous for engaging in protest activity online, though not exclusively online. They have their roots, though, on this image board called 4chan . . . a site that allows for unfettered discussion. Much of it is topic based; there are different forums related to things like fitness and travel. But there's one forum in particular, /b/, which is a forum that encourages anything and everything.

[That is] where the current idea, the current manifestation of Anonymous, was born. And one of the interesting things about 4chan is that you post anonymously, and this kind of helped solidify an existing ethic that is very committed to anonymous speech and political organizing. But for many years the name [Anonymous] was used simply for trolling and Internet pranking.

**Green:** What do you mean by "trolling"?

**Coleman:** [Trolling] can mean many different things; it's a number of activities where you're being purposefully provocative to get a reaction from someone else. And that might mean something kind of mundane, like using offensive, funny language, to more coordinated acts of trolling where people are targeted and humiliated beyond belief.

[Th]e name Anonymous, with a certain iconography, headless man, and jargon was used to kind of troll individuals online and offline. And then lo and behold, in 2008, there was an interesting metamorphosis where the name was also used to engage in activism.

**Green:** So there was not as much overt political activity before 2008?

**Coleman:** There were these very incipient moments where, for example, a racist radio personality, Hal Turner, was targeted. And he was targeted in an act of trolling, but because he was a kind of racist radio personality, people saw the politics involved and I think also saw the potential for their own power. But I think it wasn't really until 2008 where the transformation was really secured. And post-2008 . . . different individuals started to take the name and the mantle to create different networks and nodes to organize politically. So [Anonymous] not only transformed, it sprouted many heads post-2008.

**Green:** When you started your research, were you already well versed in a lot of the Internet slang or did you have to pick it up as you went along so that you could become more of a part of the group?

**Coleman:** You know, I knew some, and Anonymous is interesting because it has elements of open source culture. [P]eople use open source software to run these IRC servers, and many people are committed to Linux, which is an open source server. And then there's, of course, the kind of cultural motifs and jokes that come from 4chan and other message boards I was familiar with. . . . And then there was just like the Anonymous stuff going on, like the internal politics—Who's who? What are they doing? And that I got a good sense of, but they are kind of cloaked in a considerable degree of mystery and secrecy, so it isn't like I got total insight into everything that was going on.

**Green:** Were you able to get a sense of who actually makes up this group? Do they fit that stereotype of, I don't know, the white guy sitting at home in his parents' basement?

**Coleman:** I met enough to say that, "Wow, I'm kind of amazed at the diversity within Anonymous." I mean it's not total diversity, it may not be the rainbow nation or something like that, but it's not simply white, young males. There are a lot of males, especially in AnonOps. Chanology was much more evenly divided between females and males. There were people from many, many different ethnic backgrounds. There was, or is, I'm actually not sure about currently, but there was a very active queer community in AnonOps. Class-wise [there's] also more diversity than you might think.

[A]nother really important point is that when I studied open source, almost everyone involved was kind of skilled technically, either as a programmer, assistant administrator, [or] net administrator. In Anonymous . . . not everyone contributing is technically skilled at all. It's much more open and participatory. It's one of the reasons why it's scaled; it's the reason why so many people feel comfortable there. And people bring many skills; sometimes it's video editing or design—those are very, very important. Just participating by organizing.

**Green:** Is there a pretty big age range of participation as well?

**Coleman:** [I]t's definitely a youth movement, where by "youth" I mean . . . from teenagehood to roughly 35. That tends to be the spectrum. There's definitely some folks who are older, but that's the spectrum.

**Green:** It always amazes me when someone who's 14 or 15 years old and they can't even drive or vote yet, but they manage to break the security of a major credit card company or bring down some government organization even temporarily.

**Coleman:** No, that's true. And you know a lot of people who are hackers acquired their skills from a very young age and that's one of the things in the book I just published. I have kind of a life history of free software developers and open source developers. And many of them learn technical skills as young as three (that was a little bit rare), but between six and 10 years old.

**Green:** What makes the current incarnation of Internet collectives different from past community forums? Is this just the natural progression?

**Coleman:** Well, when it comes to open source, it's not something that simply happens online.... [G]eeks and hackers tend to congregate in major cities like São Paolo or Sydney or San Francisco. They live together. They work together. They marry. They hang out online. They see each other frequently in a kind of mundane way. They go to developer conferences. Currently there's a very big conference in Germany, the Computer Chaos Club.... A lot of hackers go and there's actually a lot of people from Anonymous who go as well, but they're not going to be public about it.

So, open source really fuses the offline and online, and it's one of the reasons why it's such a kind of robust world of technical production, of identity production. Anonymous, again, is very unusual, especially the networks that engage in illegal activity, because they can't really meet in person as much. People do become friends, . . . but they have to protect themselves and it creates some very difficult kinds of conditions.

[The] kind of large-scale protest activity we see with Anonymous that is organized primarily online is not unprecedented; this has been happening ever since the web has existed. But at this scale, richness, and depth, it is kind of new. And it's also interesting because, while Anonymous isn't pure chaos—it's got its logics and stabilities—[but the aim of anonymity] does prevent forms of routinization and institutionalization that you see, for example, with open source software.

**Green:** What is the buildup like before an operation takes place? Is there some sort of community discussion. Does someone just take a lead? What actually happens?

**Coleman:** Every operation is different . . . but there's only really a handful of possible scenarios. So, in the scenario where you have doxing, the identification and revelation of an individual, it's usually only a few people who take that initiative.... It can't happen publicly because ... in some cases it's just flat-out illegal; in other cases [it] would spark a lot of controversy within Anonymous.

In some instances someone does propose a kind of idea. This happened with Operation Payback, the second one in support of WikiLeaks, when MasterCard and other financial services pulled the plug. It was really one person who kind of, I think, tweeted something, started talking on IRC, [then] people with botnets, ... kind of compromised computers that really help with a distributed denial of service [DDOS] attack [wherein a website is taken down by a coordinated attack by many computers whose traffic actually overwhelms the site's server], started to get involved. But so many people were supportive.... [It] was a very classic example of something where an idea is proposed and everyone jumps aboard.

Operation BART is another great example.... In San Francisco, the Bay Area Rapid Transit was going to shut off cell phone access in the stations to thwart protests against police brutality. Anonymous got wind of this, started to produce videos, an IRC channel, and it got a wellspring of support, so much that they even did street protests. So it's just kind of different in every case, but definitely when it's full-on illegal, it tends to happen behind the proverbial closed doors ... in secret IRC channels or among a few people who are communicating securely.

**Green:** So we've talked a lot about operations that seem political. Should Anonymous be understood as a political entity?

**Coleman:** I think it should. And obviously the name can be used for different purposes, although I will say since 2008, but especially since 2010, it's been used pretty much exclusively for activist operations. People may not always agree with the nature of the operation, but the trolling campaigns, for reasons that are not even entirely clear to me, have kind of waned. So there have been activist operations, political operations (again, some controversial because they pertain to or use doxing or hacking tactics). .... They're tapping into some deeper disenchantments, and people are using the mantle to engage in activist causes.

**Green:** I've been fascinated at the people who have basically no interest in the Internet who hold up Anonymous as some sort of gold standard for political organizing.

**Coleman:** Yeah, I think they became a symbol of movement. . . . While there's people, certainly, who have more influence and power [within Anonymous], their whole iconography, their whole ethics, it's built on this premise of keeping hierarchy at bay, not having a leader. Occupy Wall Street was really committed to that, so it became kind of a handy symbol to adopt for that precise reason. And perhaps it sounds a little bit cheesy, but [Anonymous became] a kind of symbol for hope, political protest, expressing dismay over the political condition.

**Green:** You talk about the importance of comedy and how central it is to these groups. How does that relate to the political?

**Coleman:** In *Coding Freedom*, my ethnography of free software developers, I was just struck at how important humor was. It was just so abundant in this world, from conversation to the level of software and code, where what's called Easter eggs, little hidden jokes, are placed inside for you to find. And I have a whole chapter trying to understand how humor relates to the hacker habitat and what it says about their commitments to cleverness and individuality. Anonymous also has a lot of humor . . . more irreverent, far more grotesque, far more offensive.

**Green:** That definitely won't surprise anyone who's visited 4chan!

**Coleman:** Exactly, it comes from the world of trolling ... [and] a commitment to "anything goes" ... speech. It's loud. It's crass. It can be very funny at times, too; it's just not always as elegant. And it matters quite a bit. . . . It's part of their historical identity. It points to the conditions of their birth. It's also important for kind of in-house group membership. . . . [W]hen you don't have to do anything but say you're Anonymous, things like humor are particularly powerful forces that bind a group together. And finally, and this pertains to many different arenas of politics, but political activity can, frankly, be extremely depressing, disenchanting. There are a lot of losses, there's not a lot of gains, and humor helps keep the spirit a little bit more buoyant.

**Green:** Does humor also attract more attention to the various operations?

**Coleman:** [It] definitely can. One of the most famous ones was Operation HBGary, which was a kind of retaliation against a security firm and researcher Aaron Barr, who claimed he had infiltrated Anonymous and was going to hand over names of key operatives to the FBI. [Anonymous] ... gutted his company servers, deleted backups, downloaded e-mails, and on IRC, on Twitter, they hacked [in] and were spewing very offensive, sometimes very funny, messages. It got a heck of a lot of attention, you know? People were just so collectively enthused by it. But unlike groups like The Yes Men who really use humor in this fine-tuned manner, Anonymous isn't always so fine-tuned. ... If you're not part of this world, you don't always totally get it.

**Green:** Did you see there being other uniting political principles outside of the goal of freedom of expression and freedom of the use of Internet?

**Coleman:** Yeah. I mean, it's elastic. ... Definitely there are bread-and-butter issues, like censorship, privacy, and surveillance encryption that really get their goat. And that's where you get the largest number of participants showing a kind of support or actually getting involved. And it doesn't surprise me. They're from the Internet; they're of the Internet; they're going to protect the Internet. ... I think some of the international operations in the Philippines, in India, in Romania really give a sense of how far and wide Anonymous can travel.

**Green:** Is there any barrier for entry to the group? I mean, could someone simply go and engage in an Internet-based action and say, "This was the work of Anonymous"?

**Coleman:** On the one hand, you know, there's strength in numbers and strength in stability. So there's existing networks and you can contribute to them; anyone can show up. Now, if you've never been on Internet relay chat before, if you've never participated in the kind of culture of Internet joking and memes, you're less likely to show up, right? It's a kind of cultural capacity sort of argument. . . . We have certain capacities and experiences and that will take us down certain paths and not others. . . . And yet, compared to something like open source, which I studied quite deeply, I dedicated a chapter to a free software project that takes up to a year to join. . . . You're tested, you go through these membership procedures, you're vetted technically, and you have to write essays about your philosophy. It's just like a whole different sort of world [with Anonymous]. It has that kind of flexibility built in—elasticity and openness—and yet, cultural capacities and experiences are going to obviously limit who is going to show up to some degree.

**Green:** How does the government treat or react to such groups—Anonymous in particular?

**Coleman:** Big fans, they love it! [Laughs] They're not the hugest fans in the world.

I mean, it's different in different places. The United States has a history of criminalizing the DDoS . . . attack under all circumstances. . . . In Europe it's not so heavily criminalized, and there's also some places, like Germany, that have pointed to the possibility of seeing it as kind of protest activity. [But] there have been major arrests across the Western world, from Romania to the Dominican Republic . . . to Chile to the United States, over DDoS, over the hacking. I think it is kind of a threatening activity in the sense that, you know, while geeks and hackers require either cultural background or technical skills and capacities, there's a heck of a lot of them in the world. . . . They're employed by corporations, by governments, by nonprofits, by schools, right? And so there's this steady flow of individuals, only a portion of whom will be attracted to political activity, but all of a sudden there's this world . . . [that's] cracked down and that's led to a number of arrests. And then finally, in the context of the United States, there's also been informants. . . . Any kind of radical activist group will likely at some point be infiltrated.

**Green:** In some of your popular writing you're critical of the way the media has characterized Anonymous. What's lacking or unsatisfactory?

**Coleman:** To me, there are three elements I'm a little unsatisfied with. One is that Anonymous is primarily about hacking and hackers. It is certainly the case that the hacking gets the most media attention. . . . But again, what's so interesting about Anonymous is how it isn't these small hacker collectives, though there are small hacker collectives within Anonymous. It's just so much bigger than that. . . . That it's not limited to [hacking] is part of its strength. . . .

The second concerns its kind of amorphousness. . . . Sometimes you read these reports and you think that [Anonymous is] just completely impossible to find. And even those journalists who have talked to [some of the hackers] describe some of their places of interaction, like IRC, as the "deep web." It's not deep; it's very easy to find. And there is this kind of sociological stability to [Anonymous]. It's still a stability that is very difficult to map; you're never going to be fully comprehensive, and it takes a heck of a lot of time to really get to know them, but it is possible, and much easier than certain criminal groups who do everything possible to remain fully hidden.

And then thirdly, some folks have, I think, rightly noted that the government is going to use the example of hacktivism or Anonymous to justify greater legislative controls regarding things like surveillance. That I can't argue with. My only point in response to that is that if

Anonymous never existed or vanished tomorrow we would still have those.

**Green:** So governments can scapegoat Anonymous for their regulations?

**Coleman:** Yeah, exactly. [But the surveillance] would happen anyway. . . . [T]here are already laws in place and activities in place that we should be extremely concerned about; things are already terrible.

**Green:** So is this a case where the media is simply buying into the mythology of Anonymous, good and bad?

**Coleman:** Honestly, actually, I've been pretty impressed . . . with a lot of journalistic reports. I think they've done a pretty good job at it. The biggest [mistake] is that [Anonymous groups] tend to be described as hackers, but that's often a kind of editorial decision. . . . I think it was much worse before. . . . Actually, almost a year ago there was a series of operations that kind of made it unmistakable that Anonymous was "about" activism. Even if it was an activism that you may not agree with, kind of irreverent and dicey, it was activism, not hoodlums. And I think that changed a lot of the reporting. And then there's a lot of reporters, such as Quinn Norton, who were really embedded, really in there, who report on it very consistently and that helps tremendously.

## PARTICIPANT PROFILE

**Gabriella Coleman** is a cultural anthropologist at McGill University. She is the author of *Coding Freedom: The Ethics and Aesthetics of Hacking* (Princeton University Press, 2013) and *Hacker, Hoaxer, Whistleblower, Spy: The Many Faces of Anonymous* (Verso, 2014).

# on digital austerity*

**NATHAN JURGENSON**

O nce upon a pre-digital era, there existed a golden age of personal authenticity, a time before social media profiles. We were more true to ourselves. The sense of who we are was held firmly together by geographic space, physical reality, the visceral actuality of flesh. Without Klout-like metrics quantifying our worth, identity did not have to be oriented toward seeming successful or scheming for attention.

According to this popular fairy tale, the Internet arrived and real conversation, interaction, and identity were displaced by the allure of the virtual—a simulated second life that uproots and disembodies the authentic self in favor of digital status posturing, empty interaction, and addictive connection. This is supposedly the world we live in now (a recent spate of popular books, essays, wellness guides, and viral content practically sneer as they make the claim). Yet

---

*This essay is adapted from "The Disconnectionists," *The New Inquiry* 22(2013). It is reprinted with the author's permission.

naysayers offer hope. By casting off the virtual and re-embracing the tangible through a purifying "digital detox," one can reconnect with the real, the meaningful—one's true self that rejects social media's seductive velvet cage.

That retelling may be a bit hyperbolic, but the cultural preoccupation is inescapable. How and when one looks at a glowing screen has generated its own pervasive popular discourse, with buzzwords like *digital detox*, *disconnection*, and *unplugging* to address profound concerns over who is still human, who is having true experiences, what is even "real." A few examples: In 2013, Paul Miller of tech-news website The Verge and Baratunde Thurston, a *Fast Company* columnist, undertook highly publicized breaks from the web that they described in intimate detail (and ultimately posted on the web). Videos like "I Forgot My Phone" depict smartphone users as mindless zombies missing out on reality and go viral. Countless editorial writers feel compelled to moralize broadly about the minutia of when one might acceptably check their phone. What all of these commenters say may mean less than the fact they feel compelled to say it at all.

As Diane Lewis states in an essay for *Flow*, an online journal about new media,

> The question of who adjudicates the distinction between fantasy and reality, and how, is perhaps at the crux of moral panics over immoderate media consumption.

It is worth asking why these self-appointed judges have emerged, why this moral preoccupation with immoderate digital connection is so popular, and how this mode of connection came to demand assessment and confession at such great length and in such great detail. This concern-and-confess genre frames digital connection as personally debasing and socially unnatural (despite the rapidity with which it has been adopted). Internet and technology use is depicted as a dangerous desire, an unhealthy pleasure, an addictive toxin to be regulated and medicated. The way the concern with digital connection has manifested in such profoundly heavy-handed ways suggests something more significant than technophobia is at play. Why do so many of us feel our integrity as humans is suddenly at risk?

————

The conflict between the self as social performance and the self as authentic expression of inner truth has roots much deeper than social media. It has been a concern of much theorizing about modernity and, if you agree with these theories, a mostly unspoken preoccupation throughout modern culture.

Whether it's Max Weber on rationalization, Walter Benjamin on aura, Jacques Ellul on technique, Jean Baudrillard on simulations, or Zygmunt Bauman and the Frankfurt School on modernity and the Enlightenment, there is a long tradition of social theory linking the consequences of altering the "natural" world in the name of convenience, efficiency, comfort, and safety to draining reality of its truth or essence. We are increasingly asked to make various "bargains with modernity" (to use Anthony Giddens's phrase) when encountering and depending on technologies we can't fully comprehend. The globalization of countless cultural dispositions had replaced the premodern experience of cultural order with an anomic, driftless lack of understanding, as described by such classical sociologists as Émile Durkheim and Georg Simmel and in more contemporary accounts by David Riesman (*The Lonely Crowd*), Robert Putnam (*Bowling Alone*), and Sherry Turkle (*Alone Together*).

I drop all these names merely to suggest the depth of modern concern over technology replacing the real. This is especially the case in identity theory, much of which is founded on the tension between seeing the self as having some essential soul-like essence versus its being a product of social construction and scripted performance. From Martin Heidegger's "they-self," Charles Horton Cooley's "looking glass self," George Herbert Mead's discussion of the "I" and the "me," Erving Goffman's dramaturgical framework of self-presentation on the "front stage," and Michel Foucault's "arts of existence" to Judith Butler's discussion of identity "performativity," theories of the self and identity have long recognized the tension between the authentic and the pose. While so often attributed to social media, such status-posturing performance—"success theater"—is fundamental to the existence of identity, Facebook be damned.

These theories also share an understanding that people in Western society are generally uncomfortable admitting that who they are might be partly, or perhaps deeply, structured and performed. To be a "poser" is an insult; instead, common wisdom is "be true to yourself," which assumes there is a truth of your self. Digital-austerity discourse has tapped into this deep, subconscious tension, and brings to it the false hope that unplugging can bring catharsis.

The disconnectionists see the Internet as having normalized, perhaps even enforced, an unprecedented repression of the authentic self in favor of calculated avatar performance. If we could only pull ourselves away from screens and stop trading the real for the simulated, we would reconnect with our deeper truth. In describing his year away from the Internet, Paul Miller writes,

> "Real life," perhaps, was waiting for me on the other side of the web browser. . . . It seemed then, in those first few months, that my hypothesis was right. The Internet had held me back from my true self, the better Paul. I had pulled the plug and found the light.

Baratunde Thurston writes,

> My first week sans social media was deeply, happily, and per-
> sonally social. . . . I bought a new pair of glasses and shared
> my new face with the real people I spent time with.

Such rhetoric is common. Op-eds, magazine articles, news programs, and everyday discussion frames logging off as reclaiming real social interaction with your real self and other real people. The *R* in IRL. When the digital is misunderstood as exclusively "virtual," pushing back against the ubiquity of connection feels like a courageous re-embarking into the wilderness of reality. When identity performance can be regarded as a by-product of social media, then we have a new solution to the old problem of authenticity: just quit. Unplug—your humanity is at stake! Click-bait and self-congratulation in one logical flaw.

The degree to which inauthenticity seems a new, technological problem is the degree to which I can sell you an easy solution. Reducing the complexity of authenticity to something as simple as one's degree of digital connection affords a solution the self-help industry can sell. Researcher Laura Portwood-Stacer describes this as that old "neoliberal responsibilization we've seen in so many other areas of 'ethical consumption,'" turning social problems into personal ones (with market solutions and fancy packaging).

Social media surely change identity performance. For one, it makes the process more explicit. The fate of having to live "onstage," aware of being an object in others' eyes rather than a special snowflake of spontaneous, uncalculated bursts of essential essence is more obvious than ever—even, perhaps, for those already highly conscious of such objectification. But that shouldn't blind us to the fact that identity theater is older than Mark Zuckerberg. It doesn't end when you log off.

The most obvious problem with grasping at authenticity is that you'll never catch it, which makes the social media confessional both inevitable as well as its own kind of predictable performance. To his credit, Miller came to recognize by the end of his year away from the Internet that digital abstinence made him no more real. Despite his great ascetic effort, he could not reach escape velocity from the Internet. Instead he found an "inextricable link" between life online and off, between flesh and data, imploding digital dualisms into a new starting point that recognizes one is never entirely connected or disconnected but deeply both. Calling the digital performed and virtual to shore up the perceived reality of life "offline" is simply one more strategy to renew the reification of old social categories like the self, gender, sexuality, race, and other fictions made concrete. The more we argue that digital connection threatens the self, the more durable the concept of the self becomes.

The obsession with authenticity has, at its root, a desire to delineate the "normal" and enforce a form of "healthy" founded in "truth." As such, it should be no surprise that digital-austerity discourse grows a thin layer of medical pathologization. That is, digital connection has become an illness. Not only has the American Psychiatric Association looked into making "Internet-use disorder" a DSM-official condition, but more influentially, the disconnectionists have framed unplugging as a health issue, touting the digital detox. Perhaps most famously, Camp Grounded bills itself as a "digital detox tech-free personal wellness retreat." Alexis Madrigal, senior editor at *The Atlantic*, has called it "a pure distillation of post-modern technoanxiety." On its grounds the camp bans not just electronic devices but also real names, real ages, and any talk about one's work. Instead, the camp has laughing contests.

The wellness framework inherently pathologizes digital connection as contamination to be confessed, managed, or purified. Remembering Foucault's point that diagnosing what is ill is always equally about enforcing what is healthy, we might ask what new flavor of normal is being constructed by designating certain kinds of digital connection as symptoms. Similar to madness, delinquency, sexuality, or any of the other areas whose pathologizing toward normalization

Foucault traced, digitality—what is "online" and how should one appropriately engage that distinction—has become a productive concept around which to organize the control and management of new desires and pleasures. The desire to be heard, seen, informed via digital connection in all its pleasurable and distressing, dangerous and exciting ways comes to be framed as unhealthy, requiring internal and external policing. Both the real/virtual and toxic/healthy dichotomies of digital-austerity discourse point toward a new type of organization and regulation of pleasure, a new imposition of personal techno-responsibility, especially on those who lack autonomy over how and when to use technology. It's no accident that the focus in the "I Forgot My Phone" video wasn't on the many people distracted by seductive digital information but the woman who is "free" to experience life— the healthy one is the object of control, not the zombies bitten by digitality.

The smartphone is a machine, but it is still deeply part of a network of blood—an embodied, intimate, fleshy portal that penetrates into one's mind, into endless information, into other people. These stimulation machines produce a dense nexus of desires that is inherently threatening. Desire and pleasure always contain some possibility of disrupting the status quo, so there is always much at stake in their control. Silicon Valley has made the term *disruption* a joke, but there is little disagreement that the eruption of digitality does create new possibilities, for better or worse. Touting the virtue of austerity puts digital desire to work strictly in maintaining traditional understandings of what is natural, human, real, healthy, normal. The disconnectionists establish a new set of taboos as a way to garner distinction at the expense of others, setting their authentic resistance against others' unhealthy and inauthentic being.

This explains the abundance of confessions about social media compulsion that intimately detail when and how one connects. Desire can only be regulated if it is spoken about. To neutralize a desire, it must be made into a moral problem requiring constant vigilance: Is it OK to look at a screen here? For how long? How bright can it be? How often can I look? Our orientation to digital connection needs to become a minor personal obsession. The true narcissism of social media isn't self-love but our collective preoccupation with regulating these rituals of connectivity. Digital austerity is a police officer downloaded into our heads, making us always self-aware of our personal relationship to digital desire.

Of course, digital devices shouldn't be excused from the moral order—nothing should or could be. But too often discussions about technology use are conducted in bad faith, particularly when the detoxers and disconnectionists and digital-etiquette police seem more interested in trivial differences in when and how one looks at the screen rather than moral quandaries about what one is doing with the screen. The disconnectionists' selfie-help has little to do with technology and more to do with enforcing a traditional vision of the natural, healthy, and normal. Disconnect. Take breaks. Unplug all you want. You'll have different experiences and enjoy them, but you won't be any more healthy or real.

# TSP tie-in

## when zombies and hipsters attack!

The third section of this book deals with one of the fundamental inquiries of scholars and the public: how and why individuals subscribe to certain groups and lifestyles. A number of big-name sociologists—such as Erving Goffman, with his works on symbolic interactionism, and Pierre Bourdieu, with his writings on habitus and cultural capital—have tried to figure out the who, how, and why of this question by looking at the reciprocal relationship between organization and culture.

Many posts on The Society Pages employ a similar analytic. One set of pieces on TSP, for instance, looks at zombies. Long an artistic vessel for social critique, zombies have been used by filmmakers to critique capitalistic greed and conspicuous consumption. They are, after all, only in it for the *braaaaains*! Or, as Dave Paul Strohecker states in the Cyborgology blog post "The Zombie in Film," the "zombie serves as a fluid metaphor for articulating our deepest cultural anxieties and social fears." But what happens when that critiquing metaphor is transformed into an object of consumption? Green's Office Hours discussion with sociologist Jennifer Rutherford about the "undying" cultural obsession with zombies covers how this fascination has spawned subcultural practices that take the zombie beyond the silver screen and into the carnivalesque worlds of zombie-inspired parades and pub crawls in which the participants unite around their unambivalent desire for "brains." In short, the zombie has gone from a niche horror-flick creature to a global cultural icon.

The universally maligned hipster also becomes a figure of sociological interest. Take, for instance, the Sociological Images post by Lisa Wade titled "Bourdieu, the 'Hipster,' and the Authenticity of Taste." In her piece, Wade reviews Mark Grief's article in the *New York Times*, which considers the social significance of the hipster by drawing on Bourdieu's concepts of cultural authenticity and capital. Wade and Grief show how hipsters use markers of taste and style (for instance, personal style, politics, and occupations) to gauge how hip they and their peers are. That is, through daily interactions with like-minded individuals, taste and style can become important symbols of status and worth. The irony of this cultural process within the context of hipsters lies in the fact that people, especially those who take pride in their own "unique" lifestyle, truly dislike being labeled hipsters.

To acknowledge that one's personal preferences are actually a product of groupthink and social location challenges simplistic, conventional ideas about authentic identities. Whether they be social performance or fashion choice, we see how these categories and claims are closely linked to the broader networks of power and inequality.

—STEPHEN SUH AND KYLE GREEN

# discussion guide and group activities

1. Before opening this book, what did you think culture was? This volume presents a number of different conceptualizations, including Kathleen E. Hull's focus on ideas, Daniel Winchester's focus on material objects and practices, and Jennifer Lena's focus on community in Chapter 3. Which is most similar to your original idea of culture? Which is the most different?

2. Just as there are many definitions of culture, there are many ways to research culture. Choose a social phenomenon (such as a trend in types of TV shows or words related to emerging technology) to investigate and consider what questions you'd like answered on the topic. What questions would you ask? What do they reveal about your personal approach to culture? By asking these questions, also consider which questions or angles you would be discarding by choosing one direction of study.

3. Winchester's chapter, "The Feel of Faith," illustrates how a sociological approach to cultural objects can change

what we think of the "stuff" around us. Likewise, Kyle Green's "Troubling Bodies" illustrates how culture can shape our experiences, even with our very own bodies. What other chapters in the volume helped you see a familiar object or practice in a new way?

4. Race and gender are two of the most commonly studied and central concepts in sociology, and they are both conceived of as "socially constructed." How do authors C. N. Le and Natalie Wilson incorporate them into their analyses?

5. Like all social constructs, culture is not static or immutable. For instance, Hull's chapter, "Same Sex, Different Attitudes," illustrates how U.S. attitudes on same-sex marriage have evolved dramatically in a few decades. Likewise, Le's chapter showcases how cultural ideals regarding beauty are constantly shifting, highly dependent on historical and geographical contexts. What are some other cultural practices or beliefs that have undergone significant, recent change? How and why do you think they have changed? (Think broadly: You could use anything from the demonization of pit bulls as pets to transgender visibility in the media for this thought experiment.)

6. What critical perspectives do the panelists bring in their analysis of Burning Man in Matt Wray's Roundtable?

How does their analysis of the annual event differ based on their respective perspectives?

7. Subcultures represented in this volume include Anonymous, pigeon racers, and Comic-Con attendees. What do you think are the key qualities that make a group a subculture? Why would anyone put so much effort into becoming a member of a subculture? Think about your own motivations for the activities in which you participate regularly.

8. Gabriella Coleman provides insight into the inner workings of the online community known as Anonymous and Nathan Jurgenson critiques the flight from the "virtual." Do you think the digital experience is different from the IRL (in real life) experience? How might either be "more authentic"?

9. Our own social characteristics clearly influence how we understand culture and the world around us. Take one chapter from this book and consider its central question— say, how do the religious interact with religious objects? How would your race, religion, upbringing, class, gender, and other characteristics or identifications change your approach to that cultural object or research question?

10. Sociologists spend a lot of time studying what people do together, but those things we do alone can be telling as

well. Which chapters in this book provide insight into what individuals do in isolation? What can a sociologist tell us about these experiences that a biographer or psychologist might not?

## featured activity 1: "it's not what you're like, it's what you like."—*high fidelity*

In Chapter 3, Jennifer Lena introduces a critical analysis of music genres and the networks and meanings that surround them. Separate into groups based on your favorite genre of music (depending on the size of your discussion group, you might be as general as country or rock or as specific as psychobilly and prog rock). Together, brainstorm to identify:

1. A definition for the people associated with your musical subculture. Consider common practices, terminology, and fashion. How do you think performers and fans learn the norms of this cultural community?

2. An exemplary song from the genre. What does the song communicate about the genre? Once you read the lyrics, note whether the message might be different from what you'd remembered from hearing the song.

3. A sociological critique of the genre. What might a social scientist see as problematic about the genre? Perhaps its fans are primarily of one socioeconomic class, gender, or

political bent or the music could be seen as glamorizing commercialism, violence, or objectification. Are there individual songs that work against those arguments?

## featured activity 2: "fashion has to do with ideas, the way we live, what is happening."—coco chanel

From the hoodie vigils held after the death of Florida teen Trayvon Martin to "Walk a Mile in Her Shoes" fund-raisers, we know that clothing can be a powerful social force. For this discussion, first write down each visible article of clothing you are wearing, including accessories, and a brief description of that item. Now, in a group of two to four, compare lists. Discuss why your lists might differ or converge and how identity is reflected in what each person is wearing. How did social expectations affect what you chose to wear today?

Second, choose one item on your list and try to tell a story of how it might have been created. Use Claudio Benzecry and Daniel Winchester's chapters, in particular, to guide your thought process. Who imagined this item and what purpose did that creator believe the item would serve? What kinds of artisans and businesspeople would be needed to make, market, and sell the item? Does the item serve a different purpose for you than what you imagine was its intended purpose?

# about the contributors

**Arturo Baiocchi** is in the division of social work at California State University, Sacramento. He studies mental health interventions in a range of institutional settings.

**Claudio E. Benzecry** is in the sociology department at the University of Connecticut. He is the author of *The Opera Fanatic: Ethnography of an Obsession* (University of Chicago Press, 2011).

**Kyle Green** is in the sociology department at the University of Minnesota. He studies gender, sport, the body, and ritual. He is the co-founder of the Give Methods a Chance podcast.

**Douglas Hartmann** is in the sociology department at the University of Minnesota. His research interests focus on race and ethnicity, multiculturalism, popular culture (including sports and religion), and contemporary American society. He is coeditor of The Society Pages.

**Kathleen E. Hull** is in the sociology department at the University of Minnesota. She is the author of *Same-Sex Marriage: The Cultural Politics of Love and Law* (Cambridge University Press, 2006).

**Nathan Jurgenson** is a sociology graduate student at the University of Maryland. He is the coauthor of "Production, Consumption, Prosumption: The Nature of Capitalism in the Age of the Digital 'Prosumer'" (*Journal of Consumer Culture*, 2010).

**Sarah Lageson** is in the sociology department at the University of Minnesota. She studies media, crime, and law. Sarah is a cohost of the Office Hours and Give Methods a Chance podcasts.

**C. N. Le** is a senior lecturer and the director of the Asian and Asian American Studies Center at the University of Massachusetts, Amherst. He is the founder and principle writer for Asian-Nation.org.

**Stephen Suh** is in the sociology department at the University of Minnesota. He studies race, ethnicity, and migration, especially in relation to Asian Americans.

**Christopher Uggen** is in the sociology department at the University of Minnesota. He studies crime, law, and deviance, especially how former prisoners manage to put their lives back together. He is coeditor of The Society Pages.

**Natalie Wilson** is a literature and women's studies scholar at California State University, San Marcos. She is a frequent contributor to *Ms.* magazine's blog and writes the "Pop Goes Feminism" column for Girl w/ Pen! at The Society Pages.

**Daniel Winchester** is in the sociology department at the University of Connecticut. He is the author of *Embodying the Faith: Religious Practice and the Making of a Muslim Moral Habitus* (Oxford University Press, 2008).

**Matt Wray** is in the sociology department at Temple University and is the editor of *Cultural Sociology: An Introductory Reader* (W. W. Norton, 2012). He has been writing about Burning Man since 1995.

# Index

Note: Italicized page locators refer to illustrations.

advertising industry
    actors of color and, 109
    24/7 dynamic in, 68
African Americans, "culture
    of poverty" rhetoric
    and, 47
*Age of Independence, The*
    (Rosenfeld), 158
Allah, 18, 20
*Alone Together* (Turkle), 202
American Psychiatric
    Association, 206
American Psychological
    Association, 104
animal relationships, human
    relationships and,
    178
AnonOps, 185
Anonymous, 181, 187
    birth of, 182
    diversity within, 184–85
    government and, 193–94
    humor and, 190–92
    media characterization of,
        194–96
    political organizing and,
        189–90
    post-2008, 183
anorexia, 87, 89, 91, 93, 94
apartheid, Million Dollar Pigeon
    Race and, 175, 176
Arbus, D., xxix
architecture projects, 24/7
    dynamic and, 66–67, 68
Asian American community,
    beauty debate in, 103
Asian American women, mental
    illness, beauty images,
    and, 104
Asian beauty
    Asian supermodels and,
        103
    white, Western standards and,
        101

Asian countries
	general racial homogeneity in,
		110
	plastic and cosmetic surgery
		in, 102–3
	white images of beauty and,
		101–2
authenticity
	digital-austerity discourse
		and, 200, 204, 205, 206
	pro-anorexic sites and, 89–91
avant-garde genres, 40

Balinese cockfighting, 175
*Banding Together* (Lena), 37
Barr, A., 191
Baudrillard, J., 201
Bauman, Z., 201
Baunach, D. M., 10
Bay Area Rapid Transit (San
		Francisco), 188
BCBG Max Azria, 57
Beastie Boys, 42
Beatles, 38
beauty
	European-based images of, 101
	globalization and idea of, 97
	promoting diverse images of,
		108–10
beauty pageants
	male gaze and, 99–100
	visual conformity and
		homogeneity in, 105

bebop jazz, 41
Bell, M., 127
Benjamin, W., 201
Benzecry, C., xix, *52, 55, 56, 60,
		63, 66*
Berry, C., 109
bigotry, Asians and, 105
Black Power movement, 79
blame frames, 82, 83
blepharoplasty, Asian beauty and,
		102
bluegrass, 37
body(ies)
	discrimination and size of, 80
	identity tied to, 75
	language about, 78–79
	nuance and types of, 93–94
Boero, N., 77, 85, 86, 87, 88, 89, 91,
		92, 93
"boomerang generation," 156
Bordo, S., 76
Bourdieu, P., 210, 211
*Bowling Alone* (Putnam), 202
Brazil
	medical trials in, 62
	shoe leather sourced in, 64
Breuer, H., 115, 116
*Brokeback Mountain* (film), 8
Bronx club, pigeon racers in,
		169–70, 172, 177–78
Brooks, M., 122
Buenos Aires, Argentina, shoe
		leather sourced in, 65

bulimia, 87, 94

Burning Man, xxi, 129–51, *131*
  categorizing, 140–46
  culture and, 146–51
  demographics of, 136–40
  playa names and, 130–33,
    134–35
  reflexivity and, 147
  spreading influence of, 142
  as temporary intentional
    community, 144

Bush, George W., same-sex
    marriage and, 3, 4

Butler, J., 202

Cadieux, V., 127

California, demographic changes
    in, 109

*California's Utopian Colonies*
    (Hine), 144

Camp Grounded, 206

Campos, P., 84

*Candy: A Century of Panic and
    Pleasure* (Kawash), 127

candy consumption, 128

Catholicism, 21

Census (Burning Man), 132, 135,
    136

Census (United States)
    racial diversity, 108–9
    same-sex couples data, 12

Chanology, 185

Chen, K., 130, 136, 141, 146

Chengdu, China, shoe leather
    sourced in, 64

Chennai, India
    OmShoes factory in, 58
    shoe leather sourced in, 64

children, of unmarried parents, 13

Chin, V., 106, 107

China
    economic reforms in, 61
    reason for shoe production in,
      61–64
    shoe factories in, 49, 50, 58, 59,
      60, 61–62, 64, 65

Chung, C., xxxi

class
    fatness and, 82
    light skin tone and, 101–2

clothing design. *see* fashion design
    and production (global)

Clupper, W., 141

Coach, 57

*Coding Freedom: The Ethics and
    Aesthetics of Hacking*
    (Coleman), 181, 190

cohort replacement effect, 6, 7, 14

Coleman, G., xxi, xxii, 181, 182,
    183, 184, 185, 186, 187, 189,
    190, 191, 192, 193, 194, 195,
    196

Comic-Con, xx, 113–24

commodity chain, 54

community-generated music
    genres, 39–40

Computer Chaos Club, 186

*Conquest of Cool, The* (Frank), 148

consumption, body prepared for, 76

Cooley, C. H., 202

Cornwell, B., 161

corpulence, 79

cosmetic surgery, in Asia, 102–3

cosplay, 113, 114, 115, 123

Crossley, N., 76

cultural life, structures of feeling and, 21

cultural/media imperialism thesis, 51

cultural production, studying at global level, 51–54

cultural shift, living alone trend as, 156

cultural sociology, xix

culture, xv

    body defined by, 77

    Burning Man and, 146–51

    globalization and, 51–54

    multiple meanings and uses of term, xvii

    sex, violence, poverty, and, 46–47

    sociological critiques of, xx–xxi

    as ways of life, xxi–xxii

"culture of poverty" rhetoric, 47

Dame B, 118

Davuluri, N., 108

decommodification, defined, 130

"deep play," pigeon racers and, 175–77

Defense of Marriage Act (DOMA), 4

Def Jam label, 42

DeGeneres, E., 8

deindustrialization, of Western countries, 61

depression, Asian American women, beauty images, and, 104

Derr, H., 118

designers, cultural sociological focus on, 53–54

digital austerity, 200, 203, 204, 205, 206, 207, 208

digital connection, pathologizing, 206

"digital detox," 200

disco, 41

disconnection, 200

discrimination

    Asians and, 105

    health and, 83

    weight-based, 79–80, 84

dislocation, 139, 150–51

distributed denial of service (DDoS) attacks, 188, 194

divorce, 13, 157

DOMA. *see* Defense of Marriage Act (DOMA)

Dongguan, China, shoe production in, 59, 62, 64, 65, *66, 69*

*Dora the Explorer, xxvi,* xxvii, xxxii
doxing, 188, 189
Duneier, M., 166
Durkheim, E., 24, 202

Eastern Europe, medical trials
    in, 62
Eastern Orthodox Christianity,
    21–34
eating disorders, 85, 86, 87, 89, 92,
    93, 94, 104
*Eating Disorders* (journal), 104
Ebens, R., 107
economic status, body weight and,
    82–83
Ellul, J., 201
*Enabling Creative Chaos: The
    Organization behind the
    Burning Man Event* (Chen),
    142
Enlightenment, 201
Eucharist, 26
experts, exponential growth in, 76

Facebook, 203
faith, feel of, 20
Fakih, R., 108
families, broadening definition of,
    13, 14
Far East Movement, 109
fashion design and production
    (global), round-the-clock
    schedule, 49–51, 53, 65–70

Fashion Institute of Technology
    (SUNY), 57
fast fashion, 63, 67–68
fat-acceptance movement, 79
*Fat History* (Stearns), 81
fatness, 79
    discrimination against, 79–80
    economic status and, 82–83
    framing of, 80–81
    medicalizing and
        pathologizing, 78
    moral failings and, 81–82, 83
    positive framing options for,
        84–85
femininity, repressive ideals of, 47
feminists, pro-anorexia
    communities and, 87
financial services, time
    restructuring and, 65–67
fishing (industrial), time zone
    differences and, 68–70
*Flow,* 200
"follow the thing" strategy, 53
food, as cultural object, 126–28
food blogs, 126–27
Forever 21, 67
Foucault, M., 202, 206, 207
"found sociology," xxv
4chan, 182, 184
fracking, 179
Frankfurt School, 201
freedom, living alone and, 158–59
French Connection, 57

Frost, J., 46
Frye, 57

"Gangnam Style" video (Psy), 109
gay men, body size discrimination
      and, 81
gay rights, greater acceptance of, 8
Geeks Out (blog), 121
Geertz, C., 17, 175
gender
      body size discrimination
            and, 81
      Comic-Con and, 115–24
      fatness and, 82
General Social Survey data, on
      same-sex marriage, 10
genre(s)
      avant-garde, 40
      as community, 39
      sociological definition of, 38–39
Giddens, A., 202
Gilmore, L., 141
Girls' Generation, 109
globalization, 202
      changeability of geography
            and, 62–63
      commodity chain and, 54
      design locales and, 54–57
      idea of beauty and, 97
      industrial fishing and, 67–70
      ironies of, 108
      light skin in Asian societies
            and, 102

local competition and, 58–59
      Million Dollar Pigeon Race
            and, 175, 177
      political economy of, 52
      production locales and, 57–61
      24/7 dynamic in, 65–68
      see also shoe design and
            production
globalization and culture
      macro-level perspective on, 51
      meso level perspective on,
            51–52
      micro level perspective on, 51,
            52–53
Global Pigeon, The (Jerolmack),
      165
global product assembly,
      temporality of production
      and, 54, 67–68
Goffman, E., 202, 210
Going Solo: The Extraordinary
      Rise and Surprising Appeal
      of Living Alone
      (Klinenberg), 155
Gould, M., 47
Green, K., xx, 47, 182, 183, 184, 185,
      186, 187, 189, 190, 191, 192,
      193, 194, 196
Grief, M., 211
Guangdong Province, China, shoe
      production in, 50, 58, 62
Guangzhou, China, shoe
      production in, 59, 60

gun violence, 46

Gurira, D., 121

Gustafson, K., 47

Guthman, J., 127

Guy Fawkes masks, 181

hackers, 186, 189, 192, 195

Hartmann, D., xxvii–xxviii, xxix–xxx

Heidegger, M., 202

Heller, S. M. (the Countess), 134, 139, 145, 150

heterosexual men, beauty pageants and, 99–100

Hiese, K., 47

Hine, R. V., 144

hipsters, 211–12

H&M, 67

homogeneity
  beauty pageants and, 99
  yellow peril and, 104–7

homosexuality, greater acceptance of, 8, 9–10, 11, 14

Honda, 106

Huie, W. Y., xxv, *xxvi*, xxviii, xxx–xxxii

Hull, K., xix

icons (Eastern Orthodox tradition), *19, 22,* 23, 24, *25, 28*
  aesthetic dimensions of, 29–30
  bodily discipline and, 33–34
  as cloud of witnesses, 24–28
  icon corners, 29
  liturgical ritual and, 26, 28
  physical adoration of, 24–26
  portability of, 28–33
  as sacred gifts, 27, 28

identity, tied to body, 75

identity performance, 204, 205

identity theory, 202–3

"I Got a Boy" (Girls' Generation), 109

Iijima Hall, C. C., 104

India, shoe factories in, 58

indigenous culture, globalization and, 51

industry-based music, 41

intentional communities, 143–44

*International Journal of Eating Disorders,* 104

International Society of Aesthetic Plastic Surgery, 102

Internet, 92, 199, 201, 203, 205

Jackson 5, 109

Japanese automakers, 106

Jay-Z, 109

jazz, 39

Jerolmack, C., xxi, 165, 166, 168, 170, 172, 173, 175, 177, 178

Jesus Christ, 18, *19,* 20, 22, 24, 26, 27, *28,* 29, 31, *31,* 32

joblessness, 42, 43

John Chrysostom (saint), 24, 27

John the Baptist (saint), 24
Joseph (saint), 27
*Journal of Nervous and Mental Disease,* 104
Jurgenson, N., xxii

Kawash, S., 127, 128
Kenneth Cole, 57
Klinenberg, E., xxi, 155, 156, 157, 158, 159, 160, 161, 162, 163
K-pop, 109

Lageson, S., xix
Lap-Band surgery, 84
Latino population, *xxvi,* xxviii, xxxii
Laumann, E., 161
Le, C. N., xx
Lena, J. C., xix, 37, 38, 40, 41, 44, 45
Lennon, J., 38
Leon, Mexico, OmShoes factory in, 58
lesbian, gay, bisexual, and transgender (LGBT) communities, same-sex marriage and, 11–12
Lewis, D., 200
light skin tone, class and, 101–2
Linux, 184
living alone
    increase in, 155–63
    limitations of, 161–62
    reasons for, 157–61

*Lollipop Chainsaw* (game), 122
*Lonely Crowd, The* (Riesman), 202
"Looking for Asian America: An Ethnocentric Tour" (Huie), xxxi

*Mad Men* (television show), 162
Madrigal, A., 206
male entitlement, gun violence and, 46
male gaze
    beauty pageants and, 99–100
    Comic-Con and, 119
Marcus, G., 53
marriage
    declining rates of, 158
    living alone and preparing for, 159
    shifting attitudes toward, 13, 14
    *see also* same-sex marriage
marriage equality, 3–14
masculinity
    gun violence and, 46
    repressive ideals of, 47
Massachusetts, same-sex marriages in, 3
"Mass Shootings and the 'Man'ifesto" (Stewart), 46
"Mass Violence and the Media" (Frost & Suh), 46
Mead, G. H., 202
media
    blame frames and, 83

people of color and, 109

same-sex couples and, 8

medical information, Internet and
        democratization of, 92

medical trials, global
        pharmaceutical companies
        and, 62

"melting pot" ideal, beauty
        pageants and, 108

memes, 193

memory, songs and evocation of, 44

Mexico, shoe factories in, 58

Milan, runway shows, 55

millennials, same-sex marriage
        and, 7

Miller, P., 200, 203, 205

Million Dollar Pigeon Race,
        173–78

misogyny, Comic-Con and, 120–21

Miss Daegu, Korea 2013
        contestants, 97, *98,* 100,
        105, 107, 110

Model, L., xxix

*Modern Family* (TV comedy), 8

Molina, M., 114

mood boards, 55

moral failings, fatness and,
        81–82, 83

Morgan, D., 24

Mormons, 144

Moynihan, D. P., 47

Muhammad, 18, 20

multiculturalism, ironies of, 108–10

music
        as community, 37, 38, 43

        industry-based, 41

        preserving, 41, 42

        scene-based, 40, 41

        as social experience, 44

musical genres
        community-generated, 39–40

        definition of, 38–39

music history, understanding,
        37–38

National Alliance on Mental
        Illness, 104

Nestle, M., 127

New Mexico, demographic
        changes in, 109

New School of Design, The
        (Parsons), 57

Newsom, G., 3

Nissan, 106

Nitz, M., 107

Norton, Q., 197

Obama, Barack, same-sex
        marriage and, 4

obesity epidemic, 78, 79
        doctor visits and, 83

        framing, 80–81

        moral panic of, 88

        public health crisis frame
        and, 79

        stigma and, 83

Occupy Wall Street, 190

OmShoes, 49, 50, 55, 57, 58, 64, 65

online trend forecasting services, 55

Ono, Y., 38

open source culture, 184, 185, 186, 187, 193

Operation BART, 188

Operation HBGary, 191

Operation Payback, 188

Orbach, S., 75, 76

Orsi, R., 34

Orthodox Christianity, 21–34

Ortyl, T., 12

overweight, 78–79, 80

Paris, Le Marais window displays, 55

Pascoe, C. J., 77, 85, 86, 87, 88, 89, 91, 92, 93

pedestrian pigeons, 168

people of color, integrating into U.S. institutions, 109

perfect feminist utopia (PFU), 118

Pew Research Center, 6, 7

pharmaceutical companies, global, 62

photographs, cultural implications of, xxxi

pigeons and pigeon racers, 165–78

Pike, S., 141

plastic surgery, in Asia, 102–3

playa names, 130–33, 134–35

Poland, medical trials in, 62

political economy, of globalization, 52

pop music, 40, 41

Portwood-Stacer, L., 204

poverty, culture and, 46–47

Powell, B., 13

Pratt Institute, 57

preservationists, music, 41, 42

pro-anorexia communities, online, 77, 85–94
    aggression levels and, 90–91
    controversy around, 86–87
    criticizing extreme aspects of, 87–88
    resource sharing, 91–92
    search for authenticity, 89–91
    sharing of medical knowledge, 92
    understanding sites, 88–89

production, globalization and locales for, 57–61

professional racing pigeons, 168–69

Protestantism, 21

public health
    fatness and, 78
    obesity epidemic and, 79, 82

Puritans, 143

Putnam, R., 202

race
  beauty ideals and, 100
  fatness and, 82
Ramadan, 20
rap, 37, 39, 41–42
"rape culture," 121, 122
R&B music, 41
Reddit, 97, 104
reflexivity, 147
religion, sociology of, 17, 24
religious community, icons as
    material mediators of, 29
religious culture, aesthetics of, 20,
    21, 34
religious life, understanding
    cultural dimensions of,
    20, 34
religious meaning and experience,
    embodied and material
    aspects of, 18, 20
religious objects, larger
    community and, 24
relocation, Burning Man and
    sense of, 151
representation (or
    representativeness), xxx
rhinoplasty, Asian beauty and, 102
Riesman, D., 202
Rodriguez, M., 121
Rosenfeld, M., 158
Rubin, R., 42
Run-D.M.C., 42
Rutherford, J., 211

Saguy, A., 77, 78, 79, 80, 81, 82, 83, 84
Sam Edelman, 57
same-sex marriage, 3–14
  bans on, 4
  declining opposition to, 7–11
  federal recognition of, 4
  Gallup poll results on, 5, 5–6
  increasing cultural visibility
    and, 8, 14
  legal recognition of, 8–9, 9
  LGBT communities and,
    11–12
  majority support for, 4
  seismic shifts in American
    public opinion, xix
San Francisco, same-sex
    marriages in, 3–4
Santana, N., 49, 50, 59, 60, 61,
    65, 66
scene-based music, 40, 41
Second Life, 132
self, theories of, 202–3
Sesame Street, 135
sex, culture and, 46–47
Shenzhen, China, shoe production
    in, 59
shoe design and production,
    56, 63
  in China, reasons for, 61–64
  confirmed samples process,
    59–61
  correction markups, 59,
    60, 61

shoe design (*continued*)
    globalization and, 49–51, *52*
    locales for, 54–57
    mood boards and, 55–56
    number of annual collections, 57
    number of lines per collection, 57–58
    prototyping, 59
    round-the-clock cycle, 65–70
    supply sources, 64–65
    trend forecasting and, 55, 56
    where design happens, 54–57
    where production happens, 57–61
Silent Generation, same-sex marriage and, 7
Silver, C., 114
Simmel, G., 202
sitcoms, Asian characters in, 103–4
skin-lightening creams, 102
SlutWalk movement, 122
Small, M. L., 47
smartphone, 200, 207
sneaker production, globalized, 62
social life, culture and, 46–47
social media, 199, 200, 201, 203, 204, 205, 208
social networks, pro-anorexia communities, 85

sociological imagination, 42
sociology
    as queen of social sciences, xxii
    of religion, 24
songs, memory and, 44
South Africa, Million Dollar Pigeon Race in, 173–78
South Korean factories, 62
South Texas polka, 37
Stearns, P., 81
Stern, J. (Wee Heavy), 132, 139, 144, 149
Steve Madden, 57
Stewart, E., 46
Strohecker, D. P., 210
Suh, S., 46, 47
suicidality, Asian American women, beauty images, and, 104
supermodels, Asian, 103
sushi market, global scale of, 68–70
sweatshop workers, 53

Taiwanese factories, 61–62
temporality of production, globalization and, 54, 65–68
Texas, demographic changes in, 109
Thailand, shoe leather sourced in, 64

*Theotokos* (or Virgin Mary), *19,* 22, 29, 30, 32, 33, *33*

time restructuring, globalization and, 65–68

Tokyo, Tsukiji market, globalization and, 68–70

Topshop, 67

totemic pigeons, 168

Toyota, 106

traditionalists, 41

trolling, 182–83, 189, 191

Tsukiji market (Tokyo), globalization and, 68–70

Tumblr, 86

Turkle, S., 202

Turner, B., 75

Turner, H., 183

Tuscany, shoe leather sourced in, 64

unemployment, 42, 43

United States

    beauty standard in, 99–100

    gun violence in, 46

    Orthodox Christians in, 21

unmarried parents, 13

unplugging, 200, 203

utopian communitarianism, 143–44

"Values and Beliefs" poll (Gallup), 9

vanishing point, 29, 30

violence, culture and, 46–47

Virgin Mary (or *Theotokos*), *19,* 22, 24, 27, 29, 30, 32, 33, *33*

virtuous cycle of production, 63

Wade, L., 211

*Walking Dead, The,* 122

"wanna-orexic," 90, 91

Weber, M., 201

weight loss, 84, 89

Weisner, T., 134

"welfare queens," fatness and discourse around, 82

*What's Wrong with Fat?* (Saguy), 78, 80

Whedon, J., 123, 124

WikiLeaks, 188

Williams, R., xvii, 21

Wilson, N., xx

Winchester, D., xix, *19, 22, 25, 28, 31, 33*

Winfrey, O., 109

women

    beauty pageants and, 99

    body size discrimination and, 81

    Comic-Con and, 115, 116

    living alone trend and, 156

    weight, economic status, and, 82–83

work schedules, globalization and, 65–68

Wray, M. (Burping Man), xxi, *131*,
        133, *133, 136*, 137, 142, *143*,
        148, *149*
*WWZ* (Brooks), 122

Yahoo!, 87
yellow peril, physical homogeneity
        and, 104–7

Yes Men, 192
Yokohama, Japan, fashion-
        forward looks in,
        55, *55*

Zara, 63, 67
zombies, 210–11
Zuckerberg, M., 205